**To Abby and Amy,**

**two rambunctious miracles**

**in the Cosmic Plan**

**Cover by Tim Hartsfield**

**Standing with his disciples on a hill overlooking Jerusalem, a weeping Jesus of Nazareth prophesies the doom of the Holy City.**

# SEEING YOUR FUTURE

*A modern look at prophecy and prediction*

**JOHN RONNER**

# Seeing Your Future

## A Modern Look at Prophecy and Prediction

## John Ronner

Published by:

Mamre Press
1301 Sherwood Drive
Oxford, Alabama 36203

**Library of Congress Cataloging-in-Publication Data**
Ronner, John. 1951-
   Seeing your future : a modern look at prophecy and prediction /
John Ronner
      p. cm.
   Includes bibliographical references.
   ISBN 0-932945-38-4 : $10.95
   1. Prophecies (Occultism) I. Title.
BF1791.R65  1990
133.3--dc20              89-71384

Manufactured in the United States of America

# Table of Contents

only two popes left... The Secret Prophecy of Fatima: Are church officials suppressing it... Error: the common thread of millennialist movements... Signs of a dawning Age of Aquarius... The birth of cosmic consciousness in today's time... The great "Global Mind Change" now transforming basic human attitudes... Humanity teetering on the brink of rescue or destruction... Can the future be changed...

wild jungle of divination techniques... Idi Amin's prophetic turtle... The stamp that foretold the future... The *I Ching*: history's most revered divination system...

Finding the hidden plan for your future... A famous German rocket scientist escapes a Soviet labor camp by using mind power... How the subconscious mind creates your future... Mind-over-matter and the poltergeist... The mind and sub-atomic reality... Is time an illusion... Controlling the subconscious to bring about your destiny... The cosmic plan... Free will versus predestination... The cosmic plan and you... The illusion of separateness...

# List of Illustrations

# The Titanic

Perhaps the one event which has most astonishingly demonstrated the reality of prophecy is the sinking of the ocean liner *Titanic*, which struck an iceberg off Canada's coast in 1912.

Consider these incredible facts, among many others:

* The British journalist W. T. Stead, doomed to die on the Titanic, seemed his entire life long to display an unconscious knowledge of his date with destiny in his writing, speech-giving and behavior. As just one example, he wrote an 1892 short story that eerily described the watery demise he would face exactly 20 years later.

* In 1898, ex-sailor Morgan Robertson went into a trance and wrote a "fictional" literary story, *The Wreck of the Titan*. In amazing detail, the story turned out to be an unintended script for the events of the disaster, down to the number of passengers, tonnage of the ship, shortage of lifeboats, and many other small details.

* Typical of the numerous strange "coincidences" piling up just before the catastrophe: Two hours before the iceberg crash, singing Titanic crew members inexplicably selected the hymn, *Hear, Father, While We Pray to Thee, For Those in Peril in the Sea*. Thousands of miles away, at that moment, the same hymn was being sung by a congregation in Winnipeg, Canada. Its minister, Charles Morgan, had earlier selected the hymn for his flock after hearing the title and vividly seeing the hymn number while in a trance-like state. Although he had never sung the hymn before, he was able to locate the music in his library and include it in his church service that night.

## Did Stead unconsciously sense his doom?

The saga of one of history's best prophesied events began as early as the late 1800s. In 1892, the ill-fated Stead unconsciously predicted his destiny by publishing a story in the *Review of Reviews* about a White Star ocean liner crashing into an iceberg in the Atlantic. In the story, the only survivor was rescued by another White Star liner, the *Majestic*. At the time Stead's story appeared, there actually was a White Star ship called *Majestic*. Its captain was Edward J. Smith. Years later, Capt. Smith was transferred to another White Star liner, the *Titanic*. He went down with his ship.

In other ways, Stead seemed to show that, on some subliminal level, he knew where his life was headed. In the 1880s, Stead published an article in the *Pall Mall Gazette* about an ocean liner of the *Titanic's* eventual size which sank in the mid-Atlantic. Stead added a note to his fiction, stating: "This is exactly what might take place, and will take place, if liners are sent to sea short of boats." Decades later, this was indeed to be a main cause of the Titanic's staggering death toll: Just over 1,500 of its 2,207 passengers died, in large part because the much-vaunted "unsinkable" ship carried far too few lifeboats.

In 1910, during a lecture, Stead imagined himself as a shipwrecked passenger crying for help in the water. While the *Titanic* was under construction, Stead took a notion in 1911 to visit the colorful psychic Louis Harmon. Harmon warned Stead that any danger to his life would come only from water "and from nothing else" and he should avoid the sea. Several months later, one year before the disaster, Harmon dispatched an urgent note to Stead warning him that April 1912 (which turned out to be the month of the shipwreck) would be a dangerous time to travel. Stead nonetheless boarded the *Titanic*, despite another letter in 1912 from an Archbishop Colley predicting the *Titanic's* demise.

## Titan and Titanic: Fiction Becomes Fact

For all the drama of the Stead story, the most amazing single incident predating the 1912 *Titanic* voyage was the 1898 publication of Morgan Robertson's novel *The Wreck of the Titan*. Writing according to a vision he saw while entranced, Robertson centered his novel around a huge steamship called the **Titan**. The fictional *Titan*, like its real-life counterpart of 14 years later, was considered unsinkable because of watertight compartments but sank all the same during the month of April after crashing into an iceberg. The *Titan* was the largest ship afloat, designed to carry almost 3,000 passengers. So was the **Titanic**. Like the *Titanic*, the *Titan* was severely short of lifeboats, causing a catastrophic death toll.

Furthermore, consider these other comparisons between Robertson's 1898 *Titan* and the real *Titanic*, which was not even to be built until years later, in 1911:

**Ship: Titan versus Titanic**

Displacement tonnage -- 75,000 vs. 66,000
Persons on the ship -- 3,000 vs. 2,207
Liner's length -- 800 feet vs. 882.5
Speed at crash -- 25 knots vs. 23
Lifeboats -- 24 vs. 20
Propellers -- 3 vs. 3

# The Disaster Nears: Prophecies Multiply

On an extrasensory level, the gloomy fate of the *Titanic* spawned increasing prophecies in 1912 as the deadly date of April 14 neared.

In late March, shortly after reserving a place on the *Titanic*, a depressed English businessman J. Connon Middleton told family members about a recurring nightmare in which he viewed the *Titanic* "floating on the sea, keel upwards, and her passengers and crew swimming around her." In the nightmares, Middleton himself seemed to be watching it all while floating in the air above the wrecked boat. About a week before the *Titanic* was to leave Britain for America, Middleton canceled his passage for business reasons, because of a telegram from New York.

Mrs. Norah K. Mathews, an 11-year-old at the time the *Titanic* sailed, became sad as her mother, Mary Keziah Roberts, a stewardess on the *Titanic*, combed her hair before leaving her behind to board the ship. The sadness was triggered by the mother's singing of a song which included the words, "Yip-i-addie-i-aye... I don't care what becomes of me..." The girl told her mother: "I don't want you to sing that song again; I don't want you to sail on the *Titanic*." The mother did go but survived the sinking.

On April 10, the day the *Titanic* set off from Britain on its star-crossed maiden voyage, the British medium V. N. Turvey stated that "a great liner will be lost." Three days later, he documented the prediction in a letter sent to a Mrs. de Steiger, saying the disaster would occur in two days. She received the letter just hours after the *Titanic* struck the iceberg on April 14.

Also on April 10, as the *Titanic* glided past the Isle of Wight in the English Channel, Mrs. Jack Marshall, standing with her family on their roof to watch the ship, suddenly grabbed her husband's arm and shouted: "That ship is going to sink before she reaches America!" Marshall, trying to calm her, parroted the line that the ship was unsinkable. "Don't stand here staring at me!" countered an angry Mrs. Marshall. "Do something! You fools, I can see hundreds of people struggling in the icy water! Are you all so blind that you are going to let them drown?" The Marshalls' young daughter Joan took all this in and later wrote about the incident in a book.

As the *Titanic* made one its last stops for passengers before embarking on the open sea, at Queenstown, a young fireman deserted, although other motives besides premonition may have been at work.

On April 12, a 14-year-old English girl woke twice in the same night in her grandmother's home from vivid nightmares. They were about a large ship whose end suddenly lowered against the backdrop of terrible screams. On April 15, the girl's uncle, Leonard Hodgkinson, was identified in a newspaper as having been a crew member on the *Titanic*. He had died.

On April 14, the *Titanic's* Capt. Smith received five warnings to slow the ship's speed because of icebergs in the area. but he ignored them all. This, despite the fact that the warnings made him uneasy. Every other ship in the vicinity, however, had stopped totally.

# The End of the Titanic

At 11:40 p.m., the *Titanic* was cruising at full speed when it struck the iceberg. Five watertight ship compartments were ripped open. The stern of the world's largest ship rose and its bow tilted downward. The packed luxury liner began to sink gradually at a sharp plunging angle.

Mostly women and children began filling the 20 lifeboats. Passengers heroically gave up seats to other passengers. At 2:20 a.m., the Titanic disappeared into the water.

Among the doomed, dying passengers screaming in the water at that moment was Col. Archibald Gracie. At the same instant, in New York City, Mrs. Gracie awoke abruptly. She heard a voice say: "On your knees and pray." As she opened a book for prayer, she saw the hymn: *For Those in Peril on the Sea*. It was the same hymn which the *Titanic* passengers and the Winnipeg, Canada church congregation had simultaneously sung only hours before.

Only about 700 of the *Titanic's* 2,207 passengers survived to be saved by the ocean liner *Carpathia*. Three American millionaires were among the dead.

The American parapsychologist Ian Stevenson, who collected much of the paranormal material relating to the **Titanic**, commented that, "as an illustration of human folly... few events could exceed the sinking of the *Titanic*."

## Emotion: the Engine of Prophecy

The *Titanic* disaster shows how great emotional events typically cause numerous prophecies, particularly when those coming emotional events pose great personal danger to individuals.

Not only does emotion appear to fuel the ESP of precognition, but as a great emotional event nears, the prophecies generally accelerate and intensify. For example, Stevenson noted that 18 of 34 prophecies about a heart-rending coal disaster that killed scores of schoolchildren in Aberfan, Wales, occurred during a four-day period immediately preceding the event. Some of the most intense visions came hours before the event.

In the case of coming tragedy, prophecies are often "a cry for help, or a last sign of life, or a signal of utter panic," in the words of psychiatrist Joost Meerloo. Prophets sense these psychic distress signals.

Well illustrating all this is the Aberfan calamity, in which a million-ton heap of coal waste fell on the Welsh Pantglas Junior School in 1966, killing 116 young children and 28 adults in the mining village.

There were various forebodings in the days before the event. They included an artist who sketched out his feeling of impending doom by drawing a human head surrounded by blackness. One Englishwoman awoke from a nightmare about suffocating in profound "blackness" while another woman dreamed about a mountain flowing down as a child ran screaming. Shortly before the disaster, a London TV celebrity canceled an upcoming comedy show about a Welsh mining village simply because he had a hunch it should not be telecast.

But saddest of all were the premonitions of little Eryl Mai Jones of the Aberfan mining town, premonitions that might have saved her life if interpreted correctly.

Shortly before the tragedy, the 9-year-old Eryl Mai blurted to her mother: "I'm not afraid to die. I shall be with (classmates) Peter and June." Two weeks later, the young girl dreamed that she had left for school but had found nothing there because "something black" had engulfed it.

Some of the most vivid prophecies came right on the eve of the tragedy. The night before, during a gathering of Plymouth spiritualists, Mrs. C. Milden suddenly envisioned a valley schoolhouse buried by a coal avalanche. She also saw a horrified boy in the midst of rescue workers who were digging for bodies. One of the workers wore a peaked cap.

At 4 a.m., on the morning of the disaster, Brighton's Sybil Brown awoke terrified by a nightmare in which a child screamed in a telephone booth and another child approached her, pursued by a black, billowing mass. At the same time, a London woman awoke wheezing for air after dreaming that her bedroom walls were caving in.

At 9 a.m. on the fateful day, as Eryl Mai left home for school, the clock at her home ceased ticking. Less than an hour later, a mass of coal waste slid down a mountain and buried Eryl Mai's school. Two days later, Mrs. Milden saw the peak-capped rescue worker she had envisioned. As for Eryl Mai, the little girl, as she had predicted, was buried between her classmates, Peter and June, in a mass grave.

## The Reach of Emotion Through Time

Even as strong emotion seems to stimulate ESP such as precognition, some parapsychologists have also suggested that powerful emotion may increase the range through time at which psychic prophets can sense a coming great event. Perhaps one of the greatest seers of all time, the French physician of the 1500s, Nostradamus, may well have prophesied the emotion-charged French Revolution of the late 1700s and the rise of Napoleon, as will be seen in a later chapter.

Some wonder whether the blind St. Odelia of the 600s may have predicted Hitler's rise and World War 2 as much as 1,200 years before their time. In two Latin letters to her brother, the prince of German Franconia, she wrote that Germany would one day be called the most warlike nation on earth. "Out of her (Germany's) bosom" would come a "terrible warrior" and "conqueror," who would originate at the "banks of the Danube." St. Odelia predicted a long war in which "the conqueror will have attained the peak of his triumphs toward the middle of the second year of hostilities." The war, she added, would involve "winged warriors" ascending to the sky "to seize the very stars and throw them down on the cities ... to start great fires."

As it turned out, the Danube River was less than 50 feet from the birthplace of Hitler, who rose to become one of history's craftiest politicians and most terrible warriors. The "long" six-year second world war saw Germany and Hitler reaching their zenith midway into the second year, as St. Odelia had suggested. After the spring of 1941, Hitler never overran another major nation. In the summer of 1941, he began his fatal Operation Barbarossa, the doomed attack on the Soviet Union. Before the world war ended, whole cities in Europe had been laid waste by "winged war-riors" whose bombing set off horrid firestorms, such as at Dresden -- perhaps the "great fires" which St. Odelia referred to.

If St. Odelia did have Hitler in mind, however, she underes-timated his slow period of decline at nine months and the number of fighting nations at 20. At any rate, she commented that this conqueror's great war "would not be the end of these wars, but the beginning of the end..."

## Prophecy: Reverse Memory?

Many psychics have described the foreseeing of the future as a mirror image of the act of remembering the past -- in which the mind moves forward rather than backward, reports the noted prophet Alan Vaughan in his book *Patterns of Prophecy*. And perhaps, Vaughan suggests, emotion affects prophecy exactly as it af-fects ordinary memory. Looking toward the past, a person's clearest, longest-lasting memories are those surrounding highly emotional events. In reverse fashion, looking toward the future, a prophet's clearest, farthest-reaching visions would be of the most emotionally charged events.

## How a Great Event Moves Through Time

In her fascinating book *Beyond Explanation*, Jenny Randles compares the movement of an event down the stream of time to that of a ship. Like a ship, which pushes out watery ripples ahead of itself and behind itself, an event coursing through time likewise sends out ripples in both directions in the form of forewarnings and afteref-fects.

The aftereffects can be emotional, as in the case of the grieving which followed the *Titanic* and the Aberfan tragedies. The foresigns can also be emotional, picked up by sensitive persons ex-periencing a range of feelings and visions. These would be the "bow wave ripples," as Randles calls them.

Two of the most emotion-charged events of modern times, sending out long-range and numerous bow-wave ripples, were the assassinations of John Fitzgerald Kennedy and Abraham Lincoln. They were two men not only tied strangely to fate but also to each other, as described in the next chapter.

At 11:40 p.m., the Titanic was cruising at full speed when it struck the iceberg. The packed luxury liner began to sink gradually at a sharp, plunging angle.

Mostly women and children filled the 20 lifeboats. Passengers heroically gave up seats to other passengers. Only about 700 of the 2,207 aboard the Titanic survived.

The British journalist W. T. Stead, doomed to die on the Titanic, seemed his entire life long to display an unconscious knowledge of his date with destiny in his writing, speech-giving and behavior.

# Kennedy & Lincoln

Abraham Lincoln and John F. Kennedy were Presidents a century apart, yet a chain of weird coincidences in dates, names, circumstances and numbers links their administrations. The numerous and uncanny coincidences have suggested to many that the death of Lincoln strangely predicted the death of Kennedy a century later.

## Lincoln and Kennedy: Strange Links

Consider first these coincidences in dates:

* Kennedy and Lincoln were elected President exactly a century apart in 1860 and 1960.
* Lincoln had previously been elected to Congress in 1847; Kennedy in 1947.
* Lincoln's vice president was born in 1808; Kennedy's vice president was born in 1908.
* Lincoln's assassin was born in 1839; Kennedy's assassin was born in 1939.

Secondly, here are some coincidences involving circumstances and names:

* Kennedy and Lincoln were well-loved northerners. Each went on to inspire the world. Kennedy and Lincoln were both known for their civil rights advocacy during a time of sectional tension among northern and southern states over how blacks should be treated. Both were over six feet tall and had been in the military.
* The draft riots during the Civil War-era 1860s were paralleled by the draft resistors during the Vietnam War-era 1960s.

13

*    Both Kennedy and Lincoln had vice presidents named Johnson, who were southern Democrats and former senators.

*    Kennedy and Lincoln each had a son die while residing at the White House.

*    Lincoln and Kennedy were both killed on a Friday. Each President was shot in the back of the head as he sat beside his wife.

*    Lincoln was shot in a theater, and his assassin fled to a warehouse. Kennedy was shot by an assassin firing from a warehouse, who then fled to a theater.

*    Lincoln was shot in Ford's Theater. Kennedy was shot in a moving Ford convertible. The particular Ford model was a Lincoln.

*    Lincoln's assassin, John Wilkes Booth, and Kennedy's assassin, Lee Harvey Oswald, were both known by three-part names and both were southerners. Both assassins were murdered by gunfire while in the custody of their captors, never making it to a trial. Booth's murderer, Boston Corbett, was eventually declared insane, while Oswald's murderer, Jack Ruby, claimed insanity as a defense. Booth had been part of a conspiracy; Oswald was under suspicion of having been part of a conspiracy.

*    Kennedy's private secretary, a person named Lincoln, warned him not to go to Dallas; Lincoln's secretary, whose first name was John, warned him against going to Ford's Theater.

*    In 1858, the Cincinnati Gazette published a letter to the editor, which made the first public proposal that Lincoln should become the Republican nominee for President in 1860. The letter also suggested that a good vice presidential running mate for Lincoln would be a former secretary of the navy, who was named John Kennedy.

Finally, consider these coincidences involving numbers:

*    The names Kennedy and Lincoln each contain seven letters as do the matching last names of their vice presidents, Lyndon Johnson and Andrew Johnson.

14

\* The names John Wilkes Booth and Lee Harvey Oswald contain 15 letters apiece.

\* Andrew Johnson and Lyndon Johnson were succeeded by Ulysses Simpson Grant and Richard Milhous Nixon, each name containing seven, seven and five letters, respectively.

# The Assassinations Foreshadowed

Kennedy and Lincoln also shared another extraordinary link, a personal sense of their approaching untimely deaths. In both cases, a host of fatal premonitions from many directions confirmed their ominous personal feelings. And in both cases, when the time for their assassinations was ripe, the deadly processes were strangely facilitated by coincidences, as will be seen.

It was not long after his 1860 election that Lincoln once looked into a mirror and was taken aback to see a double image of himself. One of the twin forms was significantly paler than the other. Lincoln interpreted this to signify that he would have health during his first term but would meet death in a second term.

In April 1865, as the Civil War was winding down and just days before his assassination, Lincoln had a premonitory dream, written down by his aide and close friend Ward Lamon after hearing the President's account of it. In the dream, Lincoln wandered from room to room in the White House, seeing no one, but hearing mournful sobbing. Finally, he came into the East Room and saw a platform bearing a corpse in funeral clothes. "Who is dead in the White House?" Lincoln asked a soldier in the dream. "The President," the soldier answered. "He was killed by an assassin!"

Lincoln's body did end up in the East Room, guarded by soldiers.

This nightmare of America's greatest President was just the climax of a series of presentiments on his part. Lincoln had told Lamon that he believed he would soar to greatness in life but be cut down by an assassin at his height. The President said his dreams had confirmed that view.

On one occasion, Lincoln mentioned to Harriet Beecher Stowe, author of the anti-slavery classic **Uncle Tom's Cabin**: "Whichever way the war ends, I have the impression, I shan't last much longer."

On the day he would die, April 14, Lincoln appeared noticeably changed to those around him. He told cabinet members: "Gentlemen, something extraordinary is going to happen, and that soon." The President went on to say that he had had three dreams of himself falling from a drifting boat into a deep, broad, rolling river. The same day, Lincoln confided to his bodyguard William Crook: "Crook, do you know, I believe there are men who would want to take my life and I have no doubt they will do it. It would be impossible to prevent it."

That evening, as Lincoln was watching the play **Our American Cousin**, Booth creeped into the presidential box on his fatal mission. The mortally wounded president died the following morning at a boarding house across the street. As Lincoln died, Secretary of War Edwin Stanton looked down and said quietly, "Now he belongs to the ages."

## Kennedy's Gathering Destiny

As with Lincoln, the prophecies surrounding John F. Kennedy's assassination on November 22, 1963 were striking -- and numerous. Some have estimated the number of premonitions at tens of thousands. As with Lincoln, Kennedy seemed to have a personal premonition of what was coming and, like Lincoln, Kennedy made particularly ominous and fatalistic remarks just before he was killed.

As early as the 1950s, the seer Jeane Dixon was predicting that a young Democrat would be elected in 1960 but die in office.

In 1962, Dr. Stanley Krippner, while on an experimental hallucinogenic drug trip with the psychedelic drug psilocybin, visualized Lincoln's statue colored black, head bowed. Lincoln's face faded out and was replaced by Kennedy's. A smoking gun lay at the statue's base, and a voice repeatedly said: "He was shot. The President was shot." Krippner's eyes opened, full of tears. Krippner documented this vision in writing and reported it to Harvard University.

Even a calendar for 1963 seemed to "prophesy" the assassination. It contained a printing error showing November 22, the day Kennedy was murdered, as a legal holiday.

The world famous evangelist Billy Graham reported that he felt so worried about Kennedy's safety in Texas that he tried to contact him to warn against any trip there. After several unsuccessful tries at reaching the President, Graham said, he let his conscious mind argue him out of further attempts.

It was clear that Kennedy himself had long been worried that he might be in peril but was resigned about his future. His White House doctor, Janet Travell, reported how she and Kennedy once passed a young boy who abruptly pointed a movie camera at the President. Kennedy was startled and became momentarily tense, but he relaxed when he realized the boy had nothing more than a camera. Kennedy said softly to himself: "I will not live in fear. What will be must be."

In the summer of 1963, Kennedy was coming out of Mass when he remarked to a journalist and friend: "I wonder if they'll shoot me in church." On another occasion, Kennedy told Arthur Goldberg that his nomination for the Supreme Court by the President should not be put off, commenting: "I don't know if another opportunity will present itself. And you'll be here a long time after I'm gone."

Indeed, a favorite poem of Kennedy's was "I Have A Rendezvous With Death."

As Nov. 22 neared, the premonitions did not let up. On Oct. 25, the British psychic John Pendragon wrote Kennedy a warning letter, mentioning Pendragon's published prediction that "an attempted assassination or worse" might be at hand. "There may be a strange turning of the Wheel of Fate, for it is just a century since... President Lincoln was shot by a madman, Booth, in April, 1865," Pendragon's prediction had stated. Pendragon received no reply.

Also in October, seeress Jeane Dixon told psychiatrist F. R. Riesenmann and author Ruth Montgomery that she had, in a vision, seen the vice-presidential plaque taken off Lyndon Johnson's door. Dixon told the pair that she had sensed that the man responsible for that happening had a name with five or six letters and two syllables. "The second letter was definitely an s and the first looked like an o..." Dixon said at the time.

**American Astrology's** November 1963 issue hit the newsstands with an article by Leslie McIntyre warning that the astrological signs in November signaled "personal danger to the head of state."

At 7 a.m. on the day of the assassination, Nov. 22, eight-year-old Ricky E. McDowell, dying of leukemia at a Columbus, Ohio hospital, woke up from a two-day semicoma. He told his mother Betty McDowell about a dream he had had that President Kennedy had died. Ricky was reassured that Kennedy was well. Ricky eventually died on Dec. 28, never knowing about Kennedy's murder later on the 22nd.

Also on the morning of the 22nd, a remark by Kennedy himself strangely predicted exactly what was to happen to him a short time later. Kennedy said: "If anyone wanted to shoot the President of the United States ... all one has to do is get on a high building someday with a telescopic sight, and there's nothing anybody can do to defend such an attempt on the President's life."

Twenty minutes before the assassination, two telephone operators in the Oxnard, California area were told by an unidentified female caller, who had apparently accidentally connected with the operators: "The President is going to be killed." The FBI was summoned, but the caller was never found.

At 12:29 p.m., shots rang out as Kennedy's limousine motorcaded through Dallas. Millions later saw an amateur filmmaker's sad footage of what happened: The smiling and waving first lady suddenly looked with concern at her husband. Kennedy reached for his throat and slumped toward her. Then, the fatal bullet exploded Kennedy's head and spun him into Mrs. Kennedy's arms.

As with Lincoln's death, America was plunged into intense grief.

As psychic investigator Herbert Greenhouse put it, "When the President of the United States is about to die, the tragedy is sensed by thousands, perhaps millions of Americans... A feeling of despair seems to grip the national psyche as if there is subliminal knowledge that the tragedy is inevitable."

# Assassinations Choreographed by Fate?

In addition to the coincidences spanning two centuries and the numerous foreshadowings of their assassinations, Lincoln and Kennedy also shared something else: Their deaths were oddly facilitated by freak happenings and by decisions which the two men themselves made.

For example, Oswald killed Kennedy not through any marksmanship. In fact, his rifle had a defective telescopic lens. Unfortunately, by coincidence, the curving motion of Kennedy's Lincoln convertible exactly compensated for that telescopic fault. As for Lincoln, one of a series of murder-facilitating coincidences was that John Wilkes Booth, picking up his mail at Ford's Theater the day of the assassination, overheard by chance that Lincoln would be at Ford's Theater that night.

Despite his conviction of coming death, Lincoln continually rebuffed advisers who implored him to beef up extremely lax security. On the night he died, Lincoln was guarded by a notoriously untrustworthy former policeman, who, by chance, happened to be away from his post drinking at a bar when Booth struck. A century later, Kennedy exposed himself needlessly in Dallas by ordering that the bubble top of his Lincoln be left open. Both Kennedy and Lincoln, incidentally, were uneasy about going to their places of death, but went, nonetheless.

## The Presidential Death Cycle

As if all this were not enough, both Kennedy and Lincoln were part of a larger, strange predictive pattern involving eight Presidents, the so-called Presidential death cycle. The cycle has spelled doom in office for all presidents elected every 20 years beginning in 1840 -- with one exception. Even the exception, Ronald Reagan, was severely wounded by a would-be assassin's gunfire within three months of his inauguration.

  * In 1840 came the election of Indian fighter William Henry Harrison, the first presidential victim. Harrison died of pneumonia a month after taking office. One of several

competing explanations for the presidential death cycle is that it began with a curse placed on Harrison by a redskin prophet. The curse supposedly came decades before when Harrison led 800 fighters to victory over several thousand Shawnee Indians in the Indiana Territory.

* In 1860, two decades after Harrison's death, Lincoln's election positioned him to be the death cycle's next victim. He was shot by the Confederate-sympathizing Booth in 1865.

* In 1880, James Garfield was elected, but the next year, a disappointed office-seeker named Charles J. Guiteau fatally shot him at a railroad station.

* In 1900, President William McKinley was elected to his second term. A year later, Leon F. Czolgosz smuggled a gun into the Pan-American Exposition in Buffalo, N.Y. and fatally shot McKinley to avenge what Czolgosz felt was McKinley's support of the rich over the poor.

* In 1920, the easygoing Ohio Senator Warren Harding was elected President. Three years later, he was a sick man after corruption scandals rocked his administration thanks to subordinates who let him down. He died in San Francisco.

* In 1940, Franklin Roosevelt was reelected to an unprecedented third term. Four years later, Roosevelt died of a cerebral hemorrhage while still in office.

* In 1960, Kennedy was elected, then gunned down three years later in a still-mysterious assassination.

* In 1980, those familiar with the death cycle riveted their attention on the newly elected Ronald Reagan. Sure enough, Reagan had hardly taken office when a would-be assassin nearly shot him to death. But Reagan survived the wounding to beat the jinx for the first time in 140 years.

Vying with the Shawnee Prophet's curse is another explanation put forward by astrologers to explain the death cycle. The astrologers cite a cyclical conjunction in the sky of Jupiter and Saturn. Astrologers consider Jupiter the planetary symbol of rulers and Saturn the symbol of termination and approaching death.

Nevertheless, there may be a larger, complementary explanation for this whole extraordinary story of Kennedy-Lincoln coincidences and presidential deaths every 20 years. The answer may lie in what has been called "synchronicity" or meaningful coincidence.

On April 14, 1865, as President Lincoln was watching the play Our American Cousin, actor John Wilkes Booth crept into the presidential box. Booth shot Lincoln in the back of the head as the horrified First Lady looked on.

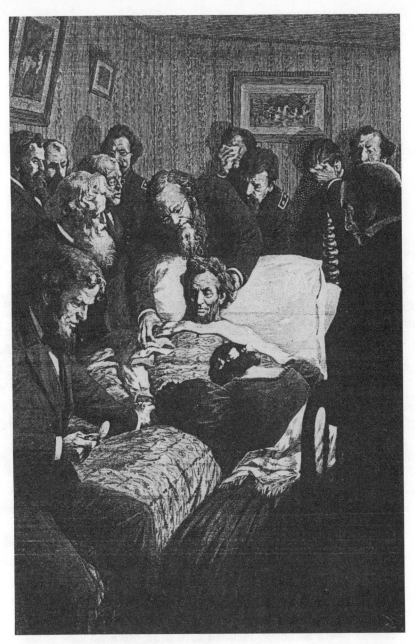

The mortally wounded Lincoln was carried to a nearby boarding house for a sorrowful vigil. When he finally died, Secretary of War Edwin Stanton looked down and said quietly, "Now he belongs to the ages."

President John Kennedy appeared to be haunted by an inner belief that he would be killed. Pictured here is an overhead view of the flag-draped presidential casket.

# Coincidence & Fate

Certainly, Lincoln's presidency could not logically "cause" Kennedy to become President a century later and behave and die so similarly. Still, the two presidencies are obviously connected. It is a coincidence with a meaning of some sort, rather than a mere fluke, a random accidental coincidence.

The world-famous Swiss psychiatrist Carl Jung noticed that the world is filled with such "meaningful coincidences," both great and small. Most of these meaningful coincidences are ignored by us. Here is another, brief example:

In 1893, Texan Henry Ziegland spurned his girlfriend. She committed suicide. The woman's brother then shot Ziegland, grazing his head, with the bullet lodging inside a tree. Assuming he'd murdered Ziegland, the brother committed suicide himself. Now, twenty years later, Ziegland decided to cut down the tree that contained the bullet. After tough going, Ziegland turned to dynamite. However, the explosion drove the tree-buried bullet into Ziegland's head, killing him.

Somehow, there is meaning in this amazing coincidence. For example, had circumstances conspired to finish the deadly business that the brother had unsuccessfully started 20 years earlier? Or is some other interpretation in order? This is the sort of meaningful coincidence that psychiatrist Jung dubbed "synchronicity."

To Jung, meaningful coincidence, or synchronicity, is a force of nature. Like gravity attracting celestial bodies to each other, this synchronistic force creates meaningful coincidences by attracting together events and people who are alike or who share roles in a common theme. But no normal cause-and-effect relationship is involved in combining the events. (Lincoln's presidency did not logically "cause" Kennedy's. Yet Lincoln's presidency and Kennedy's did share common themes, and the two presidents were alike in important ways.) To look at it another way, synchronicity puts events together into a real-life story much like a dreaming mind creates a story. The waking synchronicity and the dream both chain together events. In both cases, the events have an overall symbolic meaning to the dreamer or to the experiencer of the real-life synchronicity. In both cases, normal cause-and-effect is ignored, even defied.

## The Umbertos: Parallel Lives

Sometimes, as in the case of Lincoln and Kennedy, meaningful coincidence can be prophetic: You can make predictions by recognizing a repeating pattern of "coincidental" events (synchronicities). Take the case of Italy's King Umberto I. In 1900, the king came to the town of Monza to attend an athletic event. But beforehand, he ate at a restaurant where he noticed that the proprietor was a virtual double of him. As the king and proprietor talked, they learned that each was named Umberto, each was born on March 14, 1844, each had been married on April 22, 1868, the wife of each was named Margherita, each had a son named Vittorio. Moreover, on the day the commoner Umberto opened his restaurant, his royal double was, meanwhile, being coronated as king.

The king was unaware that they had ever met before. But the other Umberto told his majesty that they had been twice decorated together for bravery, in 1866 and 1870. On the latter occasion, the noble Humberto had been promoted to corps commander, the peasant Umberto promoted to sergeant.

During the athletic meet the next day, the king sent for his double, having decided to honor him. but the king learned that his double had been accidentally shot to death earlier that day. Just then, an assassin appeared and shot the king to death. The meaning or theme behind the coincidences? Certainly, whatever happened to the king on a grand level, could be expected to happen to his commoner "twin" on a humbler level, right up to the last moment.

Often, synchronicity harps on a particular meaningful theme, bringing about the same kind of story line or event over and over again, as with Lincoln and Kennedy or the king and his twin. It

26

is like a novelist who sticks to the same kind of formula plot in book after book, even though the stories themselves are technically different.

# The Inescapable Man

Consider the recurring theme in the story of a certain Monsieur Deschamps, reported by Jung. As a boy, Deschamps received a piece of plum pudding from a Monsieur de Fortgibu. A decade later, Deschamps noticed plum pudding in a Paris restaurant, asked for it, but was told that a diner, the very same Monsieur de Fortgibu, had already ordered it. Many years later, at a party, Deschamp was invited to eat some plum pudding as a special delicacy. Deschamp wryly remarked that the only thing missing was Monsieur Fortgibu. At that instant, Jung writes, "the door opened, and an old man in the last stages of disorientation walked in -- Monsieur de Fortgibu, who had got hold of the wrong address and burst in on the party by mistake."

As meaningfully-related patterns repeat themselves like reworked movie plots, they tend to gather power, bringing about more repetitions of the theme or the formula script, like a habit forming as the same act is repeated over and over. Jung called such habitual themes "archetypes." These archetypal themes, like basic story lines or basic ideas, are stored in the great group mind of the whole human race to be rehashed again and again in individual lives.

(Think of humanity's group mind in this way: Your individual mind is connected to the group species mind like the dim consciousness of one of your trillions of cells is connected to your individual mind. Jung called the species mind the "collective unconscious.")

All of our subconscious minds are merged together at the deep unconscious level of the species mind (like different springs merging underground at the same pool). And so we all have telepathic access to these collectively stored scripts and habitual ideas (archetypes). We use these "scripts" sometimes to unconsciously plot our lives, like playwrights.

One such great theme or "archetype" is the age-old idea that the hero who lives dramatically, mastering every situation, must die like a hero. In fact, various observers feel that this recurring theme or archetype is exactly the kind of "role" which Lincoln and later, Kennedy, were "acting" out. In so doing, they were borrowing an age-old "script" kept in storage by the human race's collective mind. They were helped along in their dramas, of course, by supporting characters, such as the two vice presidents named Johnson, and the two assassins, who fittingly were born exactly 100 years apart in anticipation of their roles "onstage."

Indeed, observers have noted that this is not the first time such a hero-must-die script has been "performed." Another hero, Julius Caesar, had a hero-must-die assassination experience that will now sound pretty familiar.

## Caesar, Lincoln and Kennedy

Like Kennedy's and Lincoln's deaths, the Roman dictator Julius Caesar's eventual demise was fraught with baleful omens and prophecies. For example, in 44 B.C., at the height of Caesar's power (both Kennedy and Lincoln had been cut down at their zenith, too), settlers accidentally exposed a tomb, which contained a plaque warning that when the tomb was exposed, a member of the Julian house would be murdered by his "kindred."

Like Lincoln, Caesar had a dramatic foreboding dream just before he was slain. The night before he was assassinated, Caesar dreamed he had died and ascended to the clouds to be welcomed by Jupiter, king of the Roman gods. At the same time, his wife Calpurnia awoke, weeping, from a nightmare in which she had held a stabbed Caesar in her arms while the walls of their home crumbled.

Like Lincoln and Kennedy, Caesar made telling remarks just before his death, suggesting that, at least subconsciously, he knew what was coming. At one point, he encountered a group which had raised the question of what would be the best death. Before anyone could answer, Caesar interjected that it would be a sudden one.

Like the heros Kennedy and Lincoln, Caesar was an intellectually keen and charismatic individual, a reformer known for greater vision than his contemporaries, adept in a wide variety of fields. For example, all three are famous for their literary endeavors, Caesar for his commentaries on the Gallic War, Lincoln for his Gettysburg Address among other works, and Kennedy for his speeches and writings, including *Profiles in Courage*, which won a Pulitzer Prize.

As with the heros Lincoln and Kennedy who followed Caesar, prophets who sensed Caesar's doom were unable to save him. Caesar brushed off a warning by the priest and augur Vestricus Spurinna that he should "beware the Ides of March" when the Roman Senate would meet. Like Kennedy and Lincoln, Caesar was warned not to go to his place of death, the Roman Senate, but like the two Presidents, he went there, anyway, though disquieted.

And like Kennedy and Lincoln, coincidences conspired to facilitate Kennedy's death. Even as Caesar was preparing to step into the Senate building, where conspirators were waiting to stab him, a warning note was pressed into his hand by one Artemidorus. But because of the crush of the crowd, he could not open it.

The facilitating coincidences are reminiscent of a screenwriter's coincidental plotting devices that help the characters guide the play to its intended conclusion. But who is the screenwriter, drawing on the archetypal story formulas for his scripts? Many students of synchronicity have concluded that the unfolding story, including the facilitating coincidences, would be the work of the group mind of all the "play's" participants, conspiring subconsciously to keep the plot intact.

Like Kennedy and Lincoln, the hero Caesar's death was greatly mourned -- for centuries, in fact. Indeed, the great medieval Italian poet Dante ranked two of the leaders of Caesar's conspiracy as among the world's three greatest sinners. Judas Iscariot was the third of the unholy trio.

As Caesar passed Spurinna on March 15 on the way to his death, he said to the priest: "Well, Spurinna, the Ides of March have come." "Yes, Caesar," Spurinna replied, "Come, but not gone." An hour later, Caesar lay dead, stabbed 26 times by a crowd of Senators who feared he was undermining the Roman Republic. That attitude probably would have met with approval by the southern-sympathizing John Wilkes Booth, who murdered Lincoln as the Confederacy, like the old Roman Republic, was collapsing.

## Science Probes the Group Mind

In recent decades, scientists have accumulated some evidence that habits of ideas or themes do form in a subconscious group species mind.

In 1981, physiologist Rupert Sheldrake sparked hot controversy among scientists with his book *A New Science of Life*, which supported that very idea. In his book, Sheldrake suggested that invisible creative fields exist. These fields, he said, govern the behavior, the ideas and even the structure of living things, including humans. Each species supposedly has its own field, which "remembers" innovations. If a member of a species learns a new behavior or has a novel idea, the field for that species changes slightly. With a changed field, it then becomes easier for other members of the species to learn the new behavior or grasp the idea. All members of the species, by being part of the collective species mind, can subconsciously and telepathically "tune into" the creative field for information. Growing embryos, for example, would "scan" the creative field "library" for information on constructing bodies and brains. In fact, a new behavior, physical structure, or idea may be adopted by so many individuals that the creative field is changed very drastically, making it far easier for even more individuals to adopt the novelty. Indeed, a critical point can be reached in the changing of the field so that the spreading novelty eventually enters the life of virtually every member of the species.

Evidence for the existence of group species minds and creative fields has cropped up. Sheldrake has cited Harvard psychologist William McDougall's startling experiments with 32 generations of rats over 15 years. McDougall laboriously trained rats to swim through a maze and avoid electric shocks. To do so, the rats had to overcome their natural inclinations and choose to swim toward darkness and away from light.

McDougall was greatly surprised to discover that each generation of rats learned the task quicker. Indeed, the 22nd generation was learning it 10 times faster. And inherited learning was not involved. Rats from untrained gene pools made the same progress. It was as if the rat species **as a whole** were learning the task.

F.A.E. Crew could not believe McDougall's research, so he organized a series of independent experiments to debunk the whole thing. However, Crew was taken aback when his rats' water maze-running capabilities began at the level which McDougall's last rats had shown. Although McDougall's first generation had needed hundreds of trials to learn the maze, some of Crew's rodents got it right the first time, with nary a shock! Australian researcher W. E. Agar got involved, too. For 25 years, Agar's similar experiments yielded the same bizarre results.

A creative field could also explain an anomaly in pigeon training: The behaviorist B. F. Skinner had to arduously train his pigeons before they would peck illuminated panels in his famous "Skinner Boxes." Today, though, researchers note that pigeons, from the first, tend to peck at lighted panels, without any extensive training. Has an archetype or mental habit for pecking lighted panels formed in the group mind of the pigeons?

## The Titanic as Archetype

So, bow-wave ripples sensed by prophets may not be the only major effect of great emotional events moving through time. In its wake, a great event may leave an archetypal pattern to be repeated (a la Caesar, Lincoln and Kennedy). In fact, the 1912 *Titanic* debacle seems to have started just such a recurring pattern.

Twenty three years after the *Titanic* disaster, in 1935, a ship called the *Titanian* struck an iceberg in the same area of the Atlantic Ocean. The *Titanian* avoided catastrophe, however, because a crew member, whose birth "coincidentally" had come on the same day as the *Titanic's* disaster, helped alert the ship's navigator before it was too late.

The *Titanic* archetype may have again spontaneously popped out of the human group mind in 1975. That year, a family in Bedfordshire, England, was watching a TV movie concerning the *Titanic's* sinking. Suddenly, an enormous mass of ice fell from clear sky above, and crashed into their roof, as reported in *The Fortean Times*. Still another in what must have been numerous archetypal sequels involved me: The day after I finished writing chapter one on the *Titanic* for this book, newspapers around the world trumpeted in banner headlines how a Soviet ocean liner had crashed into an iceberg (later dubbed a large ice floe) in -- where else? -- the North Atlantic. Fortunately, all aboard were rescued.

## Synchronicity and RFK

Abraham Lincoln and John Kennedy may not have been the only American "heros" to die amid synchronistic coincidences. Alan Vaughan, one of the world's top prophets, believes he has spotted another synchronistic web linking John Kennedy, his assassinated brother Sen. Robert Kennedy, and slain civil rights leader Martin Luther King.

In spring 1968, shortly after King's assassination, Vaughan began to get a strong premonition, supported by dreams, that presidential candidate Robert Kennedy would be assassinated. Kennedy, as the charismatic leader of the Democratic Party's progressive wing, had become another American "hero."

Synchronicity, meaningful coincidence, further bolstered Vaughan's sinking feeling about RFK. On April 19, Vaughan noticed that the main story of the Paris edition of the *New York Herald Tribune* concerned the FBI's manhunt for Martin Luther King's presumed assassin, Eric Starvo Galt (one of James Earl Ray's aliases). Coincidentally, the next column on the front page had a different article about two persons meeting violent fates. So, both side-by-side articles referred to a total of three victims of killing and violence, one of them MLK.

Next, Vaughan moved his eyes across both stories, over all eight columns of the page, as if reading the different stories together. The columns had the following suggestive phrases in this sequence:

Dr. King, killed by a single bullet/ Both were hit.../ ...Kennedy.../believed dead.../Two more Americans...and/ ...the former president.../ from the north.../ ten weeks.../

Vaughan felt that this was a synchronistic message meaning that John Kennedy, "the former president from the north" would be followed in assassination death by "two more Americans," Martin Luther King and Robert Kennedy, in "10 weeks" -- that is, by late June or early July.

King had already died on April 4, so that left RFK.

On April 29 and again on May 28, Vaughan documented his premonitions by writing letters to parapsychologists asking that Kennedy be warned. In his warnings, Vaughan noted one of several synchronistic patterns linking the two Kennedys and King: "The initials of the three, KKK, would be symbolic of the racialist fever in the U.S.," Vaughan wrote. Vaughan's warning was filed in the Central Premonitions Registry, a clearinghouse for documenting prophecies.

Vaughan's premonitions and synchronicities about RFK were seconded by the presentiments of others. In one notable case, just hours before RFK was killed on June 5, West Virginia psychic Jeanne Gardner entered a hotel and tearfully told a crowd of booksellers that Kennedy would be assassinated early June 5 in a kitchen. She said a voice had told her that the assassin would be short and swarthy, and she heard the words "Tirhan, Tirhan."

Like his brother John and MLK, Robert Kennedy was cut down by the gunfire of an assassin, Jordanian immigrant Sirhan Sirhan, as he had reached a peak in his political career, devoted in large part to civil rights. Kennedy was murdered on the night of perhaps his greatest political victory, a win in the nation's largest presidential primary in California, his fifth win in the six presidential primaries he had entered.

## Does History Repeat Itself?

Can analyzing past archetypal patterns allow us to roughly project the future course of nations, as some believe? History, they assert, literally repeats itself, although not exactly. Looking back at Lincoln and Kennedy, some observers have wondered if a heroic personality will be elected to the American presidency in 2060 during a time of national civil rights tension, only to die tragically after winning the world's admiration? And would the second president to succeed the slain hero be beset by massive scandal in his administration, as Presidents Ulysses Grant and Richard Nixon both were?

On a larger scale, Vaughan has pointed out that Great Britain has often been compared to ancient Athens, another naval empire with far-flung colonies that were lost after a devastating war (Democratic Athens' Peloponnesian War with militaristic Sparta versus Democratic Britain's World War II with militaristic Nazi Germany). Vaughan notes that Athens and later Britain both lost superpower status but kept their famed wisdom as the "university of the world."

As Athens and her rival Greek city states yielded center stage to the Romans, who lay to their west, Britain and her European rivals have been supplanted by westward-lying America. America, in her turn, has frequently been compared to the Roman Republic and Empire.

Vaughan notes, among others, such synchronistic Rome-America parallels as:

* Enforcement of a worldwide peace by deploying internationally distributed armies (Pax Americana versus Pax Romana).
* The United States rejected the idea of a king, as did the Romans, and created a republic of associated states.
* Debased coinage.
* Signs of moral decay tempered by a hardy minority resisting decadence.

In fact, drawing on these themes, Vaughan has projected a series of predictions. For example, he has forecast that Eastern cults and religions might be expected to become more and more influential in the U.S., leading to a new religion of Eastern and Christian ideas. (Some think that the New Age movement could be part of this process unfolding). Certainly, an extraordinary variety of cults and eastern religions did sweep through the Roman Empire, and one of them, Christianity, eventually supplanted the old Roman state religion.

Vaughan also sees a synchronistic link between Rome's struggle with the barbarians to her east and north and America's Cold War struggle with the Soviet Union of the east and north. If the pattern holds, America would eventually ally herself with the Soviets as Rome did with the barbarians (in staving off the Huns, for example.) Is the Soviet leader Gorbachev's *glasnost* the first sign of this?

Vaughan also predicted a more and more enveloping American welfare state, and grander and grander media events. This would all relate synchronistically to the Roman "bread and circus," the free grain doles and bloody entertainment spectaculars which kept the city poor pacified.

## Beyond Time and Space

One of the hardest things to accept about Sheldrake's creative fields or Jung's archetypes is how they can transcend time and space, popping up here and there telepathically over the many centuries.

Surprisingly, physicists in recent decades have come upon evidence that subatomic particles, such as protons or electrons, may routinely break time and space barriers to get information about each other. This has made some observers wonder whether the same thing may be happening in our larger world as well, as McDougall's rat experiments indeed suggest. In the subatomic world, two particles which have once interacted can become much like telepathic twins: One particle will instantly react in its behavior to what the other does even if the two are a universe apart. It is much like the cases of identical twins, separated at birth, who are later found to have chosen the same type of job, same model car, and are living with wives and children who all have the same first names. Like the presidential twins Lincoln and Kennedy, it seems that one twin particle "knows" what the other has been doing and acts in a corresponding way.

35

Fortuna, the matronly Roman goddess of good luck, balances herself on a globe. Its turning symbolizes the constant coming and going of happiness and misery.

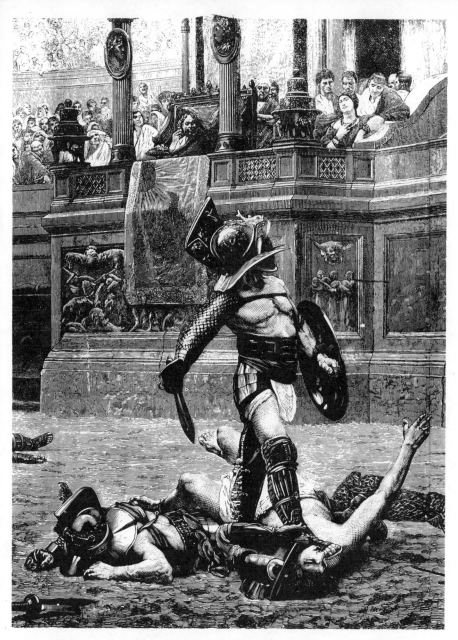

Do America's violent media spectacles and its enveloping welfare state for urban poor correspond synchronistically to the ancient Roman "bread and circus?" Pictured above: a gladiator in the Roman Coliseum.

**Was Caesar's assassination a synchronistic forerunner of Lincoln's and Kennedy's?**

# Doom or Dawn?

As our millennium winds down, tens of thousands of evangelical Christians believe they see signs that a doomsday, probably nuclear, is soon to come, prophesied by the Bible. They say two of three major Bible prophecies signaling the end of the world have recently been fulfilled: The return of the world's scattered Jewry to Israel, and Israel's uniting of all Jerusalem under its rule in 1967. These two developments set the stage for the third and final prophecy, that a Third Jewish Temple will be built in Jerusalem. Many conservative Christians say a radioactive doomsday will follow. Finally, Jesus Christ will return to earth to begin a thousand-year heavenly reign.

Meanwhile, a completely different viewpoint is shared by tens of thousands in the so-called New Age movement, which blends eastern and western religious ideas. This movement sees signs of its own that humankind is now more or less peacefully evolving upward into a "new age" of harmony, love and understanding, and a greatly higher consciousness. This progress will be free of direct divine intervention and could well avoid any nuclear cataclysm. Primarily, the New Agers cite, as their signs, the delegitimizing of war, and mass movements for ecology, democratic reform, and spiritual development, among other things.

Caught in the middle is the general population. Many are convinced that whichever scenario is right, if either is, our five-thousand-year-old civilization, just now becoming technological, faces the greatest crisis in its history. What follows is, first, the argument for a horrible Armageddon in our lifetime, and then the counter-argument for a peaceful, dawning "Age of Aquarius" already upon us.

# The Case for Armageddon

Many conservative Christians consider the young nation of Israel a yardstick for deciding how close the end times are. The return of the world's scattered Jewry to their ancient Palestinian homeland through the Zionist movement of the 1800s is considered a Biblical prophecy fulfilled and the beginning of the end of history.

The second fulfilled prophecy in the countdown to Armageddon, they say, was Israel's capture of Arab East Jerusalem during the 1967 Six Day War. That conquest united the holy city under Israeli rule and put the 2,000-year-old ruins of the Second Temple in Jewish hands. This, it is believed, will enable Israel soon to fulfill another Bible prophecy by building Judaism's Third Temple on the demolished site. (The previous two temples had been razed by Babylonians in 586 B.C. and by Romans in 70 A.D. as Jewish revolts were crushed.) The problem with rebuilding the Third Temple is that the would-be construction site is already occupied by one of Islam's holiest shrines, the 1,300-year-old Dome of the Rock. The Dome of the Rock would have to be torn down, all to the fury of Israel's antagonists, the Arabs. Building the Third Temple will supposedly be the third and last major step to doomsday.

Other signs of the "latter days" which conservative Christians say they see in current events are atheism, the Christian gospel preached worldwide, the trend toward an eventual one-world government, and growing decadence.

After the Third Temple is built, a period of horrible wars will break out just before Christ returns to earth, Bible prophecy warns. 2,500 years ago, the ancient Hebrew prophet Ezekial predicted that a northern country called "Magog" would lead an alliance of northern nations in an attack on Jerusalem during this apocalyptic period, but, Ezekial added, the massed armies would be annihilated. Many conservative Christians today consider the Soviet Union to be Ezekial's Magog. Curiously, Ezekial specifically names Persians, Ethiopians and Libyans as Magog's allies. This brings to mind the fact that Iran, once progressive, is now ruled by moslem extremists while Libya and Ethiopia, until recently monarchies, have fallen under Marxist influence.

40

The Bible's Book of Revelations paints a symbolic picture of the natural disasters supposedly to strike the earth during this so-called "Time of Tribulation." They include locusts with men's faces and wearing golden crowns swarming and torturing the sinful; four angels commanding 200 million troops to slaughter a third of earth's population; and the notorious Four Horsemen of the Apocalypse turned loose, among other plagues.

After plagues and disasters strike the earth, the Antichrist, the great evil opposite of Christ, will appear, marking the beginning of the last seven years of human history, according to Bible prophecy. Many millennialists believe the Antichrist will be a brutal international dictator claiming to be a new Messiah and persecuting any who refuse to worship him and carry his mark. The defeat of Magog (Soviet Union?) in Israel will supposedly be followed by a globally ruinous war between the Antichrist's troops and a 200-million man army led by the "kings of the east" in an invasion of the Middle East, according to Bible prophecy. Some evangelicals identify the "kings of the east" as China and her allies. The East-West war will climax in a cataclysmic battle at Armageddon, located in a plain just southwest of the Israeli port of Haifa.

Finally, snatching the faithful believers directly up to heaven, Christ will personally intervene to end the world's holocaust. He will lock Satan in a bottomless pit, resurrect the dead martyrs, obliterate the mortals who supported the Antichrist and start his earthly Golden Age reign, according to the Biblical scenario.

# End of the Popes?

The millennialists who see apocalyptic Bible prophecies being fulfilled in today's Middle East have support from many medieval and modern seers, who claim to have sensed extraordinary changes around the year 2000 A.D. One of these seers was history's greatest secular prophet, Nostradamus. Nostradamus apparently correctly foresaw the French Revolution, the empire of Napoleon and possibly the rise of Hitler. (More on Nostradamus later). Nostradamus pegged 1999 as the year of Armageddon and noted that in July of that year, a terrible Arab leader will destroy Paris from out of the sky.

Meanwhile, another medieval seer whose 850-year-old vision of future popes has been amazingly accurate over the centuries, has foretold the end of the papacy during end-of-the-world turmoil in a few more years. In 1139, during a pilgrimage to Rome, Archbishop Malachy O'Morgair claimed to have seen in a vision all of history's 111 future popes. He described each pope, in historical order of appearance, on a list of Latin mottos. Many of these mottos have been uncannily telling of the historical person they were later seen to represent. Ominously, though, St. Malachy's list of popes has almost run out. Only two future popes are left. During the reign of the last pope, St. Malachy predicts, Rome will be destroyed and "the dreadful judge will judge the people."

As an example of the accuracy of St. Malachy's mottos, consider the one he wrote for Clement XIII (1758 to 1769), whom he called the "Rose of Umbria." As it turned out, Clement had been based in Umbria, Italy, before becoming pope. Umbria's emblem was the rose. Pope Gregory XVI was known as "From the Baths of Etruria." Gregory, as it happened, had belonged to an Etrurian order before he became pope. As pope, Gregory sponsored an archaeological investigation of ancient baths in Etruria. Recent examples of St. Malachy's accuracy include Pope Paul VI, the "Flower of Flowers" whose coat of arms was the flowery fleurs-de-lis, and the very short-lived Pope John Paul I. St. Malachy called John Paul I "From the middle/half moon." It happened that John Paul died after just 31 days in office -- midway between two full moons, his job "half" completed.

Disturbingly, only two popes are now left on St. Malachy's list. These two are to follow the currently reigning John Paul II. They are individuals described by St. Malachy as "From the Glory of the Olive" (an olive branch, maybe, suggesting peacemaking?) and "Peter of Rome." St. Malachy writes of the last pope: "In the final persecution of the Holy Roman Church, there shall sit Peter of Rome, who shall feed the sheep amid great troubles. When these have passed, the City of the Seven Hills (Rome) will be destroyed, and the dreadful judge will judge the people."

# The Secret Prophecy of Fatima

Stirring up more millennialist fever has been a strange story that began on May 13, 1917 as three children were tending sheep outside the impoverished Portuguese village of Fatima. Ten-year-old Lucia dos Santos and her cousins Francisco Marto, 8, and Jacinta Marto, 7, suddenly spotted in the air above them an amazingly beautiful, brilliantly shining 16-year-old girl. She identified herself as coming from heaven. On the 13th day of each succeeding month, the children continued to meet with the apparition. Spectators showed up, becoming more and more numerous as the months passed. Only the three children could see or hear the apparition, although some claimed to see a bright cloud where the children said the apparition was located.

On July 13, as 4,500 looked on, the apparition uttered two prophecies to the children, unheard as usual by the crowd. The first one the children revealed. But the second prophecy, a suspected doomsday prophecy, has been kept secret for years by the hierarchy of the Catholic Church.

In the first prophecy, the shining girl stated that the then-raging World War 1 would end, but that another war could come when Pope Pius XI died. In fact, World War II broke out in 1939, the year Pius died. The first prophecy also warned that a powerful, unknown light in the night sky would signal the coming of this second great war, which would be a divine punishment for humankind's continued transgressions. Some religious observers have assumed that this prophesied light was an unusually bright aurora lighting Western Europe's night sky for two hours on January 25, 1938. It was so brilliant that mail carriers in the Alps made their rounds without artificial light. Some weeks later, Hitler's Nazis marched into Austria to annex it to the Third Reich.

The apparition noted that the second great war might be averted if Russia were converted away from Communism. "If not, Russia will extend her errors (in other words, Communism) throughout the world, provoking wars and persecutions against the church... Several nations will be annihilated. In the end, however, my Immaculate Heart will triumph; Russia will be converted, and the world will enjoy a period of peace."

43

Then, there was the matter of the second prophecy on that July day. The children secretly told that prophecy to church officials, and it was carried under seal to the pope. Since then, the Vatican has declined to make the prophecy public. By one account, Pope John XXIII supposedly read the secret prophecy in 1960 and was reportedly deeply shaken. In 1963, the publication *New Europa* published what was claimed to be the contents of that prophecy. The published account, which has never been declared genuine by the pope, has the apparition speaking of the greatest punishment to humankind since Noah's Flood. It is supposedly a great war to befall the race in the late 20th Century after the period of peace that follows Russia's conversion.

On Oct. 13, 1917, around 70,000 spectators were on hand in a steady downpour of rain when the teen-age apparition again appeared outside Fatima and identified herself to the children as Our Lady of the Rosary. During this meeting, a freak event witnessed by the tens of thousands present occurred after the rain suddenly stopped and the sun appeared in the sky. Eyewitnesses reported that three times the sun began wildly gyrating in the sky. At last, it plunged to earth in a zigzag motion. The terrified crowd of thousands dropped to its knees in prayer. But the sun stopped short and resumed its normal behavior in the sky. After that, the crowd realized that its previously drenched clothes and surroundings were now dry.

The apparition was eventually recognized by the bishop of Leiria as being that of Mary, Christ's mother, and a church was built at the site of the children's visions. Francisco and Jacinta, whom the apparition stated would soon be brought by her to heaven, died during the following two years in a worldwide influenza epidemic.

## A Chorus of Doomsayers

The above dismal litany is just a sampling of a vast chorus of psychic and religious doomsayers, with their eyes on the end of the millennium. Among their number may well be Robert Nixon, a retarded plowboy of the 1400s nicknamed the Cheshire Idiot, whose stunningly accurate prophecies drew the attention of England's king.

Nixon foresaw that England will one day be invaded by a country whose soldiers have "snow on their helmets." The last invasion was by the Normans in 1066.

Meanwhile, Edgar Cayce, the most famous American psychic of the 20th Century, flatly declared that World War III will break out in 1999, wiping out civilization in a year's time. For her part, Washington seeress Jeane Dixon, famous for her premonitions of Kennedy's assassination, has said she learned in a vision that the Antichrist was born in 1962 and has grown up in an Arab country.

# The Case for Aquarius

As grim and compelling as is the case for Armageddon, the case against Armageddon, many believe, is just as persuasive. Consider these points:

*       To begin with, many major prophets confidently predicting doomsday around 2,000 A.D. have been spectacularly wrong with many other predictions. Jeane Dixon, for example, said the Chinese would start an international war in 1958 and that the Russians would win the race for the moon. Even the great Nostradamus was terribly vague in his predictions, using symbolic and scrambled language, because, he said, the politics of his day required disguised predictions.

*       The doomsayers disagree with each other. Nostradamus, for example, has scheduled the end of the world for no earlier than 2038 at the least.

*       If medieval and modern seers have been sensing "bow wave ripples" of a coming holocaust, they may have tuned into one of the cataclysms already experienced in this troubled century, such as World War II and the massacre of the Jews by the Nazis.

*       The alleged Fatima doomsday prophecy, if such it is, and St. Malachy's true-to-the-mark papal mottos may well be pointing to a **possible** future, not an inevitable one. Indeed, the Fatima apparition spoke explicitly of the pos-

sibility of changing the future to avert World War II. (We will see later how evidence indicates that the future can be changed).

*     Many of the end-of-the-world prophecies may well be drawing their contents from a millennial *archetype* -- a great, recurring idea in the species mind that the world should logically end at the close of the second Christian millennium. But an archetype is not the same as a "bow wave ripple" of a coming event, although an archetype can become a self-fulfilling prophecy. Specifically, the apparently genuine Fatima miracles behaved much like a mental archetype, a classic Catholic idea of how the blessed Virgin Mary should be. As if scripted by a Catholic archetype, the Fatima events perfectly matched the religious expectations of those participating in the miracles. Mary appears, archetypally, as a teen-age girl, holding a white rosary in hands folded in front of her breast, suspended in the air, etc. A prophesied doomsday for sinful humanity, if indeed it occurred, would further fit the archetype. (In the same way, UFOs have always mirrored the changing archetypal expectations of the public. UFOs graduated from being airships in the 1890s, to "Foo Fighters" in World War II, flying saucers in the post-war era and now, motherships, as that particular archetype of alien visitation has evolved in the collective human mind). The danger of millennialism as a powerful archetype is that, as we have seen with Kennedy and Lincoln and the presidential death cycle, archetypes can gell into reality. They can even facilitate "coincidences" which bring about their realization as self-fulfilled prophecies. The brighter side, though, is that only one fraction of Christendom is mentally participating in this millennialist archetype with their collective mind power. Billions of other Christians and non-Christians have other mental expectations for the end of the century or none at all. In fact, for most of the world, not using the Christian calendar, the end of the Christian millennium in 2,000 A.D. will be just another year according to their dating systems. And the various Christian ideas about Third Jewish Temples and so

on are, to millions of these people, a complete mystery. Will their non-millennialist archetypes "cancel out" the creative power of the pro-millennialist thinking?

## Israel: Self-fulfilled Prophecy?

All this brings us to the very arresting fact that the Jews have returned to Palestine, have seized the ruins of the Second Temple and are indeed poised to build a third one, all in dramatic accord with Biblical prophecy. Nevertheless, these things have been a consuming passion for the sons of Abraham ever since they were scattered over the ancient world. Some observers wonder whether this is really a case of an inevitably self-fulfilling prophecy, the power of a great collective idea that could not be stopped.

## Error: The Millennialist Trademark

Error has been the one common thread running through millennialist movements that have broken out in just about every generation since the crucifixion of Christ. Part of the reason is mostly vague Bible prophecies, which have been ingeniously interpreted to fit each generation's situation. Even Christ himself is ambiguously quoted about when and how the Second Coming should take place. In the Gospel of Mark, he is quoted as saying quite explicitly that the end times would be a physical doomsday and would come in the lifetime of his contemporary followers. On the other hand, the Gospel of Luke quotes Christ in one place as instructing the Pharisees that the Second Coming would be symbolic, not literal and physical -- that is, an inner, spiritual revolution of higher consciousness, not a concrete Armageddon. "The Kingdom of God does not come in such a way as to be seen," Jesus said, when asked about the Second Coming. "No one will say, 'Look, here it is!' or 'There it is!;' Because the Kingdom of God is within you."

So, the Armageddon-Aquarius debate was already somewhat under way as Christianity began. In the meantime, there have been countless passionate but failed end-of-the-world movements:

\*       In 988, the Christian world supposedly took it as a terrible omen when a wolf entered the cathedral at Orleans and seized a bellrope in his mouth to ring out the death toll of the world as the first millennium wound down. Thousands of psalm-singing pilgrims made for the Holy Land in preparation for the end in 999.

\*       In 1179, the astrologer John of Toledo said the end would come in 1186 when all the then-known planets gathered in the constellation Libra. There was an uproar all over Eurasia. The Byzantine emperor ordered his palace windows shuttered.

\*       In 1524, more than 20,000 Londoners fled their city for higher elevations after astrologers predicted that doomsday would begin on Feb. 1 with a flood of London.

\*       One of the strangest apocalyptic movements centered around Sabbatai Zevi, a Jew who convinced thousands of his fellow Jews in the Mediterranean world that the end was coming in 1666 and that he was their Messiah. Commerce stagnated as Jewish merchants lost interest in trade. Zevi led a band of followers in a march on the capital of the Turkish Empire to begin his apocalyptic rule. But instead, Zevi was arrested by the Turks. The shrewd, ruling sultan was careful to spare Zevi and deny him any martyrdom. Instead, the sultan ingeniously managed to convert Zevi to Islam, and Zevi's movement fizzled out!

\*       After poring over the Bible, New York's William Miller, a stammering self-taught Baptist, became convinced that doomsday was coming sometime around 1843. A spectacular meteor shower in 1833 helped his cause along. Miller eventually pegged Oct. 22, 1844 as a doomsday date. Millerites, some in white robes, waited by the thousands on New England hilltops to be lifted to heaven. One man, wearing turkey wings, tried to fly from a tree but fell and broke an arm. On that exciting day, a Millerite spotted an unflustered Ralph Waldo Emerson, the great philosopher, and a companion of Emerson's taking a casual stroll. Asked by the Millerite if they knew the end was coming, Emerson's companion noted: "It doesn't much concern me. I live in

Boston." Emerson chimed in: "The end of the world doesn't bother me. I can get along without it." The Millerites wept when nothing happened, and called it "The Disappointment."

* Just a generation ago, Indian astrologers proclaimed that a particular conjunction of eight planets in the sky spelled doom for the earth on Feb. 2, 1962. Millions of Indians prayed. In one rite, more than a ton of butter and thousands of flowers were sacrificed. 250 priests started a relay to repeat Hindu liturgy 4.8 million times.

## Is Aquarius Upon Us?

The idea of a loving and peaceful Age of Aquarius gradually dawning now for mankind was first widely publicized in the 1960s. At that time, astrologers noted that the point in the sky where the sun is at the beginning of spring had been in the constellation Pisces for the last 2,000 years. But, they said, that point (the spring equinox) is now shifting into Aquarius, signaling the beginning of a new age, governed by Aquarian qualities of harmony and spiritual growth. These qualities are in contrast to the previous traits of the outgoing Age of Pisces. (This shifting in the sky occurs because the earth, as it rotates, also wobbles like a top in a 26,000-year cycle, moving the spring equinox through all the constellations of the zodiac. Some astrologers considered 1960 as the year of the shift to Aquarius. 1960, coincidentally, was the beginning of the counterculture decade of the 60s. It was a time when, suddenly, large numbers of people had a new vision of a saner, more enlightened world. Many of the peace-seeking, spiritually oriented "flower children" of the 1960s became part of the New Age movement of the 1970s and 1980s, a movement which today is still rapidly growing worldwide. It embraces a bewilderingly diverse number of self-transforming ideas and practices, ranging from mental healing and yoga to health food, martial art discipline and mystic vision quests.

International developments which New Agers would see as supporting their idea of a dawning Aquarian age include:

*       A respiritualization of the materialistic Western world, helped by a massive influx of eastern ideas and mystical teachings which are synthesizing with the best of Western theology. This cross-pollination is uniting science and religion, east and west on a higher level, they say. All over the developed world, millions of sophisticated individuals are attaining a universalist spiritual outlook. This melting pot theology combines the basic truths which all religions share while abandoning their dogmas and biases.

*       The liberalization of Communist bloc nations. This would include, among other things, Soviet leader Mikhail Gorbachev's *glasnost* ("openness") reforms, Hungary's decision to democratize itself and to tear down its part of the Iron Curtain, Communist Poland's first-ever competitive elections, and the struggling pro-democracy movement in China.

*       A strange, sudden but welcome worldwide outbreak of peace and conciliation in the late 1980s. This includes the Soviet pullout from Afghanistan, the Vietnamese withdrawal from Cambodia, the banning of intermediate range nuclear weapons in Europe, the settling of a brutal war in Namibia (Southwest Africa), and peace between Iran and Iraq. At this writing, the military in the Sudan has overthrown a civilian government in order to intervene and stop a horrible civil war raging for years between Arab moslems and black Christians and animists. These are only a few examples. All this coincides with a general delegitimizing of war in the average person's mind. To consider how drastically public attitudes toward war have changed, consider the fact that in 1914, the outbreak of World War I was greeted by celebratory dancing in the streets of European capitals.

*       The mushrooming environmental and antinuclear movement, including such organizations as the green parties of Europe, Greenpeace activists and the like. The growing tendency of individuals to see themselves first as citizens of the planet, and only secondly as citizens of various nations. Consider the global cooperation in curbing destruction of the ozone layer.

# The Birth of Cosmic Consciousness

Some observers feel that the above developments -- and many others like them -- are signs that humanity could be in the first stage of a great evolutionary leap from self-consciousness to cosmic consciousness. In his classic 1901 book *Cosmic Consciousness*, Richard M. Bucke explains the difference. In higher mammals and humanity, he wrote, simple consciousness, such as that of a frog, has evolved into an awareness of the self. But Bucke said that so far, only a handful of humans have attained cosmic consciousness, the highest form of awareness. In cosmic consciousness, the individual directly feels his identity as merged with the whole universe, which is perceived as an undivided, gigantic, loving organism intending good for all its interconnected parts. The self includes everything and everything is included within the self. Cosmic consciousness brings a staggering leap upward in moral sensibility, intellectual power to understand the purpose of the universe, and strong emotions of triumph and ecstasy. It makes a person "almost a member of a new species," as Bucke put it. Bucke believed that the tiny human elite attaining this higher consciousness has included Jesus of Nazareth, Paul of Tarsus, the Buddha, Mohammed, the Italian poet Dante and the American poet Walt Whitman. But he said many others experience fleeting moments of this exalted state of consciousness, popularly called a "mountaintop experience," which nonetheless alter their lives for decades. As evolution progresses, those moments will become more frequent and longer lasting in more individuals until one day, cosmic consciousness will be universally present, Bucke said.

In his engrossing 1983 book *The Global Brain*, Peter Russell suggests that the number of persons involved in raising their consciousness through active spiritual programs may currently be increasing exponentially, though their population is still small at present. Of 500 persons whom Russell interviewed who were involved in inner growth, 40 percent had started their work within the previous four years, Russell reported. Russell predicts that a coming "Consciousness Age," will supplant the bygone Industrial Age and the current post-industrial Information Age. The Consciousness Age will be a time when the average person's prime effort is geared to spiritual growth because his economic and information wants have already been satisfied by progress. In the Consciousness Age, "people would be as familiar with meditation and spiritual experiences as today they are familiar with pocket calculators and cassette tapes," Russell writes.

## Global Mind Change

Reinforcing other signs of an "Aquarian Age," a growing chorus of commentators is arguing that a radical, gigantic shift is under way in Western society's basic world view, now 300 years old. Longtime futurist and author Willis Harman calls this shift in philosophy a "global mind change." Harman's and others' ideas vary, but the argument frequently goes like this: Around the 1600s, the scientific revolution turned the world upside down. The new scientists contradicted thousands of years of ancient wisdom by teaching that man was nothing special in the cosmos. Indeed, the universe was just a big, precise, soulless machine which appeared by accident and has no purpose. Human beings also appeared by accident, and were like little machines themselves, without souls and without a purpose, according to the new philosophy. There was no God and no immortality, no psychic phenomena, since nothing really exists except the physical world. This bedrock materialist philosophy soon came to be mirrored in society's drive to blindly exploit the natural world's resources to build what is, admittedly, an unprecedented level of Western materialist prosperity.

Materialist attitudes arose as more was learned about the workings of the world in the late Middle Ages. Early scientists, for instance, proved that the earth was not at the center of the universe, among many other ancient debunked religious ideas. Until the late 1800s, the continuing surge in knowledge bolstered the materialist philosophy. But then, the tide began to turn as new data came in, particularly in physics. Physicists soon were showing that, in the subatomic world, reality has a ghostly, peek-a-boo nature, quite alien to the materialist scenario.

Meanwhile, materialism further came under attack because of the vast social problems the philosophy was creating. The idea of a soulless, purposeless universe has frequently been blamed for the spiritual barrenness and nihilism of the 20th Century Western world. Also, this "progress"-oriented philosophy has been blamed for the increasing unthinking rape of the natural environment, most disastrously seen in the systematic destruction of the earth's "green lungs" -- the huge Amazon rain forest -- and in the thinning of the earth's protective ozone layer.

Many observers say a quiet but powerful shift has recently been under way in humanity's basic world view. The shift is away from atheistic materialism and irresponsible individualism. It is toward a new global philosophy embracing mysticism, social responsibility, and individual empowerment. In the new philosophy, the universe is usually regarded as a united, living, knowing organism with a destiny and purpose. The universe is not just dead, accidental, fragmented matter. Humanity is the deliberate creation of this conscious universe, and we also have a purpose. Moreover, the physical world itself is an illusion created by the universe's consciousness, the so-called "cosmic mind" (like the species mind, but on a vaster scale). Some say the physical world is merely a working laboratory for human beings to play out their roles for the spiritual and intellectual development of their immortal souls, a learning process that continues well beyond physical death. Even separateness is an illusion, and all of fractured creation is really seamlessly united on a very fundamental level, which mystics in their deep meditations have contacted in every age.

"We are already well into the mind change," writes Harman. "It is altering the way we interpret science; it is drastically modifying our concepts of health care; it is revolutionizing our concepts of education," causing far-reaching changes in the business world, "delegitimizing war, and causing a total rethinking of the means of achieving national and global security."

# Humanity on the Brink

If a global mind change is occurring, is it, like Hollywood's cliche cavalry, arriving at a gallop just in the nick of time? Millennialist and Aquarian alike often agree that our race stands at a dangerous crossroads in its history, environmentally and atomically. As Buckminster Fuller put it, "The world is now too dangerous for anything less than utopia."

Beginning on New Year's Eve, 1986, hundreds of millions of people began joining each other worldwide in a yearly mass prayer and meditation for world peace and harmony called the World Healing Meditation. This interfaith meditation, involving more than 500 million in 82 countries in 1987, occurs on the same date at a synchronized time across the 24 time zones. Participants send out feelings of love and mentally picture the planet as harmonious. Behind the mass meditation is the belief that focusing so much mental power on a single idea can actually change reality at a time of critical global need. Some feel that what is actually happening is a gentle altering of the human species mind, specifically the species mind's "creative field" for peace consciousness (a strengthening of the peace archetype, to put it another way). This would be much like the way McDougall's maze-trained rats helped untrained rats "learn" the same maze decades later. When millions think regularly and concentratedly on peace, the argument goes, the species mind is changed so that it supposedly becomes "easier" for any given individual -- or political leader -- to become peaceful in his own thinking. As the archetype for peace is strengthened, "coincidences" which facilitate peace and harmony should suddenly start appearing, in the manner of the coincidences which tragically helped along Kennedy and Lincoln's archetypal deaths. Indeed, some supporters of the mass meditation idea claim credit for the curious coincidental outbreak of peace and goodwill in international relations in the late 1980s on an amazing variety of fronts (See the examples above). In one recent example, the Cuban dictator Fidel Castro startled the USA with an apparently serious, about-face offer to help fight drug trafficking and had a national military hero sentenced to death for just that. In the words of the late archbishop of Canterbury, William Temple: "When I pray, coincidences tend to happen; when I don't, they don't."

In 1979, two meditating groups of 3,000 each in Amherst, Mass., and Fairfield, Iowa, took part in an experiment to see if mental states could be psychically transferred. Neither the groups nor the experimenters knew exactly when mass meditation was going on. Yet the brain-wave activity of the Iowa group was found to be more synchronized whenever the Massachusetts group was meditating.

"The important point is that ... one person's general state of consciousness appears to set off similar, though generally weaker, effects on other people. This implies that as more and more people in society start experiencing such (higher) states of consciousness, other people will gradually pick up the effect, making it easier and easier for them also to reach such states," writes Russell.

## Can the Future be Changed?

Even if a nuclear doomsday were coming upon us, rather than some other destiny, our future is not fixed but can still be changed, many students of prophecy believe. They see the unborn future as consisting of tendencies that become stronger as time goes on. Evidence that a probable future can be thwarted is seen when a prophecy almost is fulfilled but not completely. The philosopher H.A.C. Dobbs has cited the case of "Lady Z," as an example. Lady Z dreamed she was riding in a coach near Piccadilly Circus, the hub of London, when her coachman fell to the street, striking his head. The next day, as she arrived at Piccadilly during a coach trip, she noticed the coachman leaning back as if his horse team was moving violently. Remembering her dream, Lady Z told the coachman to stop. She jumped from the carriage with her child and summoned a policeman to catch the wobbling coachman. Just as the policeman intervened to help, the coachman fell. Without Lady Z's quick action, the coachman apparently would have injured himself as in her prophetic dream.

Whether Armageddon, Aquarius or a different future looms, humanity today seems precariously poised at a critical juncture. And the prophet Ezekial's words may be fitting for us: "He who takes warning will save his soul."

In the end times, the Four Horsemen of the Apocalypse are released from heaven to devastate the earth, according to the apocalyptic vision of John the Divine, recorded in the Book of Revelation. Shown above is the horseman Death.

In the Book of Revelation, following the horrible end times and the last judgment, John the Divine is shown the New Jerusalem, an utopian city in which God and mankind now live together, no longer separated.

Sir Isaac Newton

Aquarius the water carrier

The Kremlin, Moscow.

**Signs of a possibly dawning Age of Aquarius include the overthrow of the materialistic Western world view symbolized by Newton and the liberalization of totalitarian Communism.**

# The Evidence

As early as the 1930s, modern science was looking seriously at precognition and getting unusual confirmations of its existence. The famed parapsychology researcher J. B. Rhine made use of a special deck of cards marked with stars, circles, wavy lines, and other patterns to detect ESP in test subjects, including prophetic abilities. Would-be prophets were asked to intuit the order in which cards would come up from a not-yet shuffled deck.

In fact, experimental card-guessing made it into the *Guiness Book of World Records*. The reference book listed the high scoring of a 26-year-old New York woman tested by Hunter College Prof. Bernard F. Reiss. The woman accurately predicted 1,349 cards in 1,850 guesses for a 73 percent rate of "hits." She correctly guessed roughly 1,000 more cards than would have been expected from chance alone.

By 1968, a pair of French scientists discovered that mice could predict which half of a cage was going to get an electric shock and avoid that space. The scientists used a machine to deliver, at random, shocks to one half of a mouse cage or the other. The mice became so adept at avoiding the shocks by moving to the safe half of their cages that they attained odds of 1,000-to-1 against chance, as reported in the September 1972 *Journal of the Society for Psychical Research*.

One of the most rigorously designed experiments to test precognition was conducted by the brilliant physicist, Helmut Schmidt. Schmidt set up a panel of four lamps which would light up at random. Which lamp would light was decided by a target-generating machine. The target generator was controlled by a process of unpredictable radioactive decay. Schmidt's test subjects attempted to predict which lamp would light up. They beat odds of a billion to one in 60,000 trials, and the master guessers turned out to be a truck driver, a housewife and a medium.

Schmidt caused another scientific stir after succeeding Rhine at Duke University's Institute for Parapsychology. There, Schmidt set up a panel of nine lamps arranged in a circle in a different experiment that was written up in conservative scientific publications. This time, the target generator, still controlled by radioactive decay, acted like a random electronic coin flipper. If "heads" came up, the panel's lights would flash one after another in a clockwise motion. If tails came up, the motion would be counterclockwise. Test subjects tried to use psychokinesis or "mind-over-matter" to will the lights to move only in one direction. In the end, fifteen subjects beat randomness significantly enough to obtain odds of 1,000 to one against chance. When the subjects were taken from the machine, it resumed a completely random operation. Schmidt observed that his results could be attributed to precognition as well as psychokinesis.

## Test Subjects See the Future

In the 1970s, a striking experiment at California's Stanford Research Institute apparently had test subjects developing, through special instruction, the ability to mentally see scenes that lay in the future. It started as a simple psychic "remote viewing" experiment conducted by physicists Harold Puthoff and Russell Targ. Puthoff and Targ taught more than 100 test subjects special techniques to help them psychically "see" remote scenes in the present -- scenes which were out of their view. More than two thirds of the subjects were then able to successfully practice the skill, the two researchers reported.

But the experiment took a tantalizing turn when Puthoff and Targ wondered if the amateur psychics could **peer into the future** during their remote viewing. Could the test subjects see scenes not only out of their view but ahead of them in time? To check this, the experimenters decided to let their subjects secretly document what they were psychically seeing. Only after the psychic descriptions were confidentially documented would the experimenters, kept unaware of what scenes were described, randomly and independently choose target scenes. Would there be a correspondence between the scenes described and the scenes later chosen as targets? This turned out to be the case. An outstanding subject was soon identified in a professional photographer, who scored four fairly clear successes in four tries. In one case, the subject described seeing a "formal garden, very well manicured." Puthoff visited Stanford University Hospital's formal garden. On another occasion, the star subject spoke of a "black iron triangle that someone had somehow walked into." Each second, she said, she heard a squeaking sound. As it turned out, Puthoff later arrived at a playground and trifled with a squeaking, triangle-shaped swing.

As far back as the 1950s, the mounting laboratory evidence for precognition and other ESP had already begun to be impressive. At that time, London psychologist H. J. Eysenck noted: "Unless there is a gigantic conspiracy involving 30 university departments all over the world, and several hundred highly respected scientists in various fields, many of them originally hostile to the claims of the psychic researchers, the only conclusion the unbiased observer can come to must be that there are people who obtain knowledge existing in other people's minds or in the outer world by means yet unknown to science."

## Precognition in the Dream Lab

Puthoff and Targ intentionally turned their remote viewing experiment into a test for precognition. But at a New York dream lab, an experiment to test a dreamer's telepathic abilities accidentally generated evidence for precognition. At the Maimonides Medical Center's dream laboratory, events began as psychiatrist Montague Ullman and psychologist Stanley Krippner experimented to see if an awake person could telepathically transmit the image of a famous painting to a dreamer. The person remaining awake concentrated all night on the painting. The results were sometimes striking. In one case, the sender concentrated on Gangin's *The Moon and the Earth*, showing a dark-skinned, nude girl beside a watery stream. Meanwhile, a sleeping secretary dreamed three times about girls who were "scantily clad." In one dream, the secretary saw herself in a bathing suit. In another dream, she saw a "dancing girl" who had "dark, tan shoulders." Then came a surprising twist. Krippner and Ullman began to notice that the sleeper frequently would not dream about the current night's painting but about a painting that would be "transmitted" on a subsequent night.

## Prophetic Dreams: Pharaoh & Twain

Some may be taken aback at the Maimonides research, but the prophetic dream actually has a long pedigree. It was universally accepted -- and honored -- in ancient times. The best-known ancient example is the case of the Biblical Joseph, sold into Egyptian slavery by brothers jealous over the fact that Joseph was favored by their father, the Hebrew patriarch Jacob. According to Hebrew legend, Joseph impressed the Egyptian pharaoh by interpreting two of the ruler's prophetic dreams. In his first dream, the pharaoh had stood at the bank of the Nile River. He watched seven fat cows appear. Next, seven lean ones appeared and ate them. In the second dream, the pharaoh had seen seven ripe ears of corn consumed by seven lean ears. Joseph told pharaoh that the dreams meant Egypt would have seven coming years of agricultural plenty followed by seven years of famine. The pharaoh took Joseph's recommendation that grain be stockpiled during the years of plenty, and he rewarded Joseph by making him his chief administrator.

In our time, Samuel Clemens, better known by his pen name Mark Twain, had a prophetic dream of his brother Henry's death, several weeks before it occurred. In 1858, Samuel vividly dreamed of seeing Henry, a Mississippi steamboat worker, lying in a casket on two chairs. The body was dressed in one of Samuel's suits. Also, an arrangement of white flowers with a single, central red rose lay on Henry's chest. Samuel told his sister about the dream. Within a few weeks, news came to Samuel that his brother's steamship had exploded, killing 150 persons and severely wounding Henry. Samuel kept a bedside vigil until Henry finally succumbed days later, and Samuel then fell into an exhausted sleep. As Samuel awoke, he saw the casket scene he had visualized in his dream, except that no flowers were present. But at that moment, a woman approached the casket and put a group of white flowers with a central red rose on the body.

On the other side of the Atlantic, the Victorian novelist Charles Dickens dreamed of a woman in a red shawl. In the dream, she said, "I am Miss Napier." Dickens did not know the woman but some hours later, two women appeared, accompanied by a girl in a red shawl who was introduced as Miss Napier.

A particularly curious prophetic dream was that of Alfred Maury, himself a dream researcher of the 1800s. Maury dreamed so vividly and panoramically of the French Revolution that he assumed he had actually somehow traveled back through time. In his dream, he was one of the insurgents but nevertheless came to be doomed to die at the guillotine. Just as the blade was to fall in his dream, Maury's real-life bedpost broke and tumbled onto his neck.

## The Doom of Flight 191

In late May 1979, office manager David Booth of Cincinnati had one of the most dramatic prophetic dream experiences in recent history. Booth's unsolicited journey into prophecy was a series of recurring nightmares, 10 nights in a row. He would hear faltering engines, then see a large, three-engine American Airlines jet moving very slowly and too quietly considering its nearness. The jet would sharply tilt, flip over onto its back, and crash on the ground amid an orange and red fireball. Every night, Booth woke up crying.

After several of the nightmares, Booth phoned the Federal Aviation Administration, American Airlines, Cincinnati Airport officials, and a University of Cincinnati psychiatrist. Booth was taken seriously and interviewed. Booth's information suggested to aviation officials either a Boeing 727 or a DC 10. But there was no practical way for the FAA to successfully fit Booth's detailed descriptions of the plane and airport with a specific aircraft and site.

"The thing that strikes me -- that always struck me -- was that it just wasn't making the noise it should for being that close," Booth was quoted as saying. After dreaming of the disaster the second time, Booth said, "I did everything to stop sleeping from then on." But the nightmares continued nonetheless until May 25.

On that day, at Chicago's O'Hare Airport, actress Lindsay Wagner, who has played the Bionic Woman among other roles, had a strong negative premonition as she and her mother were about to board a three-engine American Airlines DC-10, Flight 191. At her insistence, she and her mother canceled their reservations, as reported by author Jenny Randles. Seconds after takeoff, one of the DC-10's engines broke off. The jet flipped over and crashed, killing all 273 aboard amid a horrible fireball. It was North America's worst aviation calamity to date.

"It was uncanny," an FAA spokesman said after the crash. "There were differences (in Booth's descriptions and the actual crash), but there were very many similarities. The greatest similarity was his calling the airline and the airplane ... and that it (the plane) came in inverted." Among other things, the crash location described by Booth turned out to resemble O'Hare Airport. After the crash, Booth's nightmares did not return.

"Why she (Wagner) was lucky and the rest of the passengers doomed is a question we cannot answer," Randles commented. "But how many of those passengers felt unusually ill at ease, or had vague premonitions upon which they chose not to act?"

## Dreams: Common Prophetic Vehicles?

The coiners of exotic words have come up with "oneiromancy" to describe the practice of foretelling the future by heeding and interpreting dreams, as described above. Indeed, oneiromancy may well be the most common way prophecy occurs. This may be because dreaming appears to be one way in which the usually non-psychic person manages to experience ESP. The commonness of dreaming as a means of prophecy is shown by a collection of around 7,500 cases of premonition over three decades by researcher Louisa Rhine. Sixty-eight percent of those premonitions occurred in dreams rather than during waking hours. With more than 700 billion dreams experienced by Americans alone each year, according to at least one reckoning, there appears to be plenty of fertile ground for prophecy.

## Premonitions Bureaus Document Prophecy

In the 1960s, a new touch was added to the scientific examination of prophecy. Clearinghouses were set up to validate prophecies by documenting them before they were fulfilled. These clearinghouses became known as "premonitions bureaus" and accepted submitted prophecies from the public. The premonitions bureaus also have sought, with little success, to develop a pool of prophets who could reliably, by patchwork consensus, serve as an early warning system for major disasters. Nevertheless, the bureaus have identified a few skilled seers and have authenticated a few prophecies in individual cases. By the end of its first year, among nearly a thousand prophecies submitted, the British Premonitions Bureau had logged four particularly on-the-mark predictions about Robert Kennedy's assassination. For its part, the New York-based Central Premonitions Registry documented an impressive premonition report from a Michigan woman, among other cases. She dreamed that white-dressed, turbaned men with slanted eyes would be associated with an American ambassador's death and with a 6-foot white fence. Two weeks after the written prophecy was logged, the American ambassador in the mostly moslem African nation of Sudan was killed. A photo of the incident depicted a tall, white fence.

Despite the successes of the bureaus, the overall accuracy rate of their registered prophecies has been low. By 1980, the Central Premonitions Agency, for example, had received around 5,000 predictions, of which only 49 were considered successful. And half of those, interestingly, came from just five persons. Even the few accurate predictions generally have made an early warning system impossible because they often lack vital details of place and time.

The idea of a coordinated approach has not been limited to premonitions bureaus, however. A California research organization called the Mobius Group has had teams of coordinated psychics trying to form consensus predictions about specific future events, among other activities. In an archaeological rather than prophetic activity, the Mobius Group gained early fame by using the consensus of psychic teams to find a lost city in Egypt and the underwater ruins of Marc Antony's palace in Alexandria, Egypt.

The prophetic dream goes back a long way. The best-known ancient example is the case of the Biblical Joseph. This ancient Hebrew rose from slavery to become the chief administrator of an Egyptian pharaoh because he successfully interpreted the ruler's symbolic dreams about the future.

The Roman dictator Julius Caesar was among the historical figures who have had prophetic dreams. The night before he was assassinated, Caesar dreamed he had died and ascended to the clouds to be welcomed by Jupiter, king of the Roman gods. At the same time, his wife Calpurnia awoke, weeping, from a nightmare in which she had held a stabbed Caesar in her arms while the walls of their home crumbled.

The Victorian novelist Charles Dickens dreamed prophetically of a woman in a red shawl. In the dream, she said, "I am Miss Napier." Dickens did not know the woman, but some hours later, two women appeared, accompanied by a girl in a red shawl, who was introduced as Miss Napier.

# Faces of Prophecy

The world of prophecy encompasses much more than the hoary bearded stooped man with the gnarled staff. The many faces of prophecy include:

    \* Unsuspecting literary prophets whose works, ranging from novels to crossword puzzles, have unintentionally predicted the future.

    \* Prophets whose visions are so vivid and three-dimensional that they resemble time warps.

    \* Animals who sense natural disasters

    \* So-called futurists, who employ not psychic power but cold, scientific logic to guess what lies ahead.

    \* The tabloid seers, known for their often zany predictions, perhaps geared more to entertaining the masses than edifying them.

    \* Ancient pagan prophets who spoke for gods and were heeded by kings.

    \* Prophets of doom, whose gloomy forecasts sometimes took centuries to be fulfilled in all their particulars.

    \* Biblical prophecies, including those of Jesus of Nazareth.

## Verne Foresees Space Shot

In the late 1800s, the Victorian father of science fiction, Jules Verne, set the standard for the literary prophet who unwittingly predicts the future. His novel *From the Earth to the Moon* (1865) and its sequel *Round the Moon* (1870) turned out to be more than just speculative fiction about moonbound spacemen. A century later, many details of these novels were bizarrely mirrored by actual events in America's Apollo moon-landing missions. This was particularly true of the first lunar landing mission, Apollo 11, and of the near-fatal mission, Apollo 13.

Here are some of the surprising similarities:

* Verne's fictional launch site was at Cape Town, Florida. The site Verne described is near the actual 20th Century launch site of Cape Canaveral, Florida.

* Verne called his cone-shaped spaceship the *Columbiad*; The Apollo command module was similarly shaped and the Apollo 13 lunar lander was named the *Columbia*. More about this below.

* As with Verne's spacecraft, the Apollo spacecraft carried three spacemen. Verne's *Columbiad* had two dogs aboard, suggestive of the dogs shot into space by the Soviet Union in the early days of the space race.

* In Verne's fiction, mathematical computations for the moon mission were performed at England's Cambridge Observatory. A century later, calculations for the Apollo missions were done at the Smithsonian Astrophysical Laboratory in Cambridge, Mass.

* Verne's *Columbiad* was to travel 25,000 miles an hour and arrive at the moon in 97 hours; Apollo 11 moved at 24,000-plus miles an hour drawing away from the earth, and this first lunar landing mission also averaged 97 hours travel time going and coming.

* Although a Frenchman, Verne's novel had the United States pioneering the exploration of space. This, despite the fact that in Verne's Victorian times, France and England were the superpowers, not America, which was then an emerging but still fledgling power.

* The food capsules eaten by Apollo's astronauts were reminiscent of the *Columbiad* menu. Verne's space travelers dined on food that was compressed by "strong hydraulic pressure" to the "smallest possible dimensions."

* The fictional spaceship and the real craft both had rockets to escape lunar orbit and reduce re-entry speed.

Most uncanny was Verne's narration of how the fictional *Columbiad* crew suffered a near-fatal disaster. The *Columbiad* was enroute to the moon when it began leaking oxygen. The spacemen were forced to give up their moon landing, but they nonetheless decided to circle the moon, using its gravity to whipsaw their crippled craft back to earth. This was strangely similar to the oxygen tank explosion which forced the outbound Apollo 13 mission to abort its moon landing but circle the moon for its own whipsaw ride earthward. The unlucky Apollo Flight 13 tempted fate from the beginning by having *Columbia* as the name of its lunar lander -- in view of the fictional *Columbiad's* fate. Moreover, Apollo 13's April 1970 launching occurred exactly a century after the writing in April 1870 of Verne's novel *Round the Moon*, which recounted the near-fatal perils facing the *Columbiad*. Ironically, on the "unlucky" 13th of April, two days after the launching, Apollo 13 suffered its oxygen tank explosion. The next day, President Richard Nixon called for worldwide prayer for astronauts James Lovell Jr., Fred Haise Jr., and John Swigart Jr. For four days, the world watched anxiously as the three astronauts coped with a power failure by using the lunar module's oxygen and power. Apollo slingshoted around the moon for a gravity push homeward while the trio of astronauts braved chilling and dropping temperatures in their spacecraft. A century earlier, Verne's fictional crew had been threatened by asphyxiation or freezing. Finally, earthbound mission control navigators guided Apollo 13 to a landing. Like Verne's spacemen, Lovell, Haise and Swigart were rescued by an American vessel after a safe splashdown in the Pacific.

Commentators have raised two ideas concerning the *Columbiad-Columbia* link. Did Verne unconsciously pick up psychic impressions from a bow-wave ripple of the coming Apollo near-disaster? Or did Verne's story, which was immensely popular internationally, become a self-fulfilling prophecy? That is, did it nurture an archetypal idea in the species mind, an archetype that gathered force until it finally congealed into reality? Whatever the explanation, if there is any, it is ironic that the very name of the Apollo mission is taken from the ancient Greek god of prophecy! Verne, however, was not a perfect prophet. His astronauts did wear Victorian-style smoking jackets and rested on 19th Century tufted velvet couches. And Verne's *Columbiad* was launched from the earth not by a rocket but blasted upward out of an immense gun barrel.

## Crosswords Reveal D-Day

Literary prophets have even used the crossword puzzle as a medium for their revelations. In May 1944, crossword puzzles began appearing in a British newspaper which revealed top-secret code words for the imminent Allied D-Day invasion of Nazi-occupied France during World War II. As recounted by Arthur Koestler in *The Challenge of Chance*, the various code words started appearing in *London Daily Telegraph* crossword puzzles about a month before the June invasion across the English Channel. On May 3, the code word "Utah," one of the Normandy beaches chosen for a landing, appeared. On May 23, "Omaha," another landing beach codeword surfaced. Then, on May 31, "Mulberry," a code name for artificial harbors to be used in the landings, appeared. To top it all, just four days before the invasion, on June 2, two major code words, Neptune and Overlord, showed up. Operation Overlord was the code name for the whole invasion. How did one of the war's most tightly held secrets get into an ordinary newspaper crossword? British intelligence wanted to know. But schoolmaster Leonard Sidney Dawe, the paper's senior crossword fashioner for decades, was unaware of the words' significance and could not explain how he thought them up. Koestler classed this synchronicity as precognition. But he said it could also be that Dawe unconsciously picked up the words telepathically from the minds of hundreds of men anxious over a vital secret.

## The Black Abductor and Patty Hearst

The interrogated crossword editor, Dawe, could probably commiserate with James Rusk Jr., the author of the novel *Black Abductor*. Rusk's 1972 novel *Black Abductor* unwittingly predicted major aspects of the 1974 abduction of Patty Hearst, one of America's most publicized kidnappings.

After the kidnapping, intriguing similarities between Rusk's literary kidnap victim Patricia and the real life Patricia became evident. The fictional Patricia was the collegian daughter of a well-known wealthy political conservative. So was Miss Hearst, whose father, Randolph Hearst, oversaw a nationwide media empire and was known for his connection to conservative causes. The fictional Patricia's kidnappers were a terrorist group led by a black. So were Miss Hearst's terrorist kidnappers, in her case calling themselves the *Symbionese Liberation Army*. The SLA was led by black convict "General Field Marshal Cinque Mtume" (Donald D. De Freeze), who presided over a tiny band of mostly white radicals. In fact as well as fiction, Patricia's boyfriend was beaten by the abductors and briefly came under temporary suspicion by lawmen. In the *Black Abductor*, the kidnapping occurred near Patricia's college, and in real life, the 19-year-old Miss Hearst was dragged screaming and half-naked from her off-campus apartment near the University of California, where she was studying art. In the novel, Patricia stopped opposing her captors and was won over by their radical politics. In real life, several weeks after her kidnapping, Miss Hearst startled the country with an underground announcement that she was joining the terrorists and had changed her name to "Tania." The fictional Patricia's father received polaroid shots of his daughter. In real life, the radical SLA released a nationally publicized photo of Miss Hearst in a revolutionary stance and carrying a weapon in front of a red SLA banner. In the real-life drama, the bulk of the SLA membership was killed in a shoot-out with police. After a 19-month manhunt, Miss Hearst and some surviving SLA members were captured.

Unwitting literary prophecies such as the above are quite common with writers. Often, however, the theme of a literary project will suddenly start manifesting, synchronistically, in the outside world while the literary work is still in progress (as with my writing on the *Titanic*; See chapter 1). The famed scholar Gustaf Davidson, for example, was writing his mammoth reference work on angels when, he said, he was confronted one day during a walk by a supernatural being, who struggled with him in a way similar to how the Biblical "Dark Angel at Peniel" wrestled with the Hebrew patriarch Jacob.

In other cases, as with Verne's *Columbiad*, a bow-wave ripple may have been picked up unconsciously by the writer or a powerful reality-changing archetype set in motion by the writer's book. Authors in these latter two categories might well include, besides Verne:

\*      The Victorian mystery writer Edgar Allan Poe. In his 1833 novel, *The Narrative of Arthur Gordon Pym*, Poe wrote about a cabin boy named Parker who was killed as a sacrifice and cannibalized by a small band of fellow, starving adult shipwreck survivors. After some years, there actually was a shipwreck in which a cabin boy named Parker was cannibalized.

\*      Jonathan Swift, the British satirist who published *Gulliver's Travels* in 1726. This witty mockery of mankind was an instant success and became a classic children's travel tale. In the novel, Swift's fictional astronomers discovered two moons circling around Mars. Swift's description of the distance of each moon from Mars and its orbital period strikingly corresponds to actual fact. Yet, the two moons, Phobos and Deimos, were not discovered in real life until 1877.

## Time Warps: Lifelike Prophecies

Sometimes a prophetic vision is so lifelike and panoramic that the visionary seems to experience a physical time warp. This, even though the psychic event actually is still only mental. British Air Marshal Sir Victor Goddard's "flight into the future" in 1934 is a case in point. Goddard had suddenly been caught in a storm and become lost as he flew his Hawker Hart biplane over Scotland. So the pilot descended to seek out a familiar landmark, the abandoned ruined Drem airfield. But when Goddard located the field, it was not covered by an overlay of clouds as were its surroundings, but nestled in a zone of bright sunlight. And instead of a decaying, abandoned airfield, Goddard saw bustling mechanics in blue overalls servicing odd-looking yellow planes among restored buildings. Strangely to Goddard, no one looked up as his biplane buzzed the airfield's hangars at an altitude of 50 feet. Having gotten his bearings, Goddard flew back into the clouds. Had Goddard looked four years into the future? In 1938, four years after his strange flight, as Europe neared World War II, the ruined and abandoned Drem field was restored and reactivated as a flying school for the Royal Air Force. Moreover, the color of the training planes, which had once been silver, was changed to yellow, as Goddard had seen them in his vision. A pilot overflying Drem in 1938 would have seen what Goddard claimed he saw in 1934.

Prophecies seem to run along a spectrum of vividness ranging from panoramic 3-D dramatizations like Goddard's to the vaguest presentiments, consisting only of unconscious feelings. The experience of the German literary genius Wolfgang Goethe, who once supposedly met his future self, reflects a "time warp" dramatization on perhaps a lesser scale than Goddard's. In his work *From My Life*, Goethe writes that he once was riding on horseback along a footpath when, "I saw myself coming to meet myself, on the same path, on horseback, but in a garment such as I had never worn... As soon as I had aroused myself from this dream, the vision entirely disappeared." Eight years later, Goethe said, he suddenly realized he was on the same road wearing the garment "which I had dreamed about and which I now wore, not out of choice but by accident."

Time warp visions have a sound-only counterpart in the *Vardogr* phenomenon of Norway. In the case of the *Vardogr*, a spouse might typically hear the familiar sounds of a mate returning home: footsteps on a walkway, certain doors opening, a cane being laid against a wall. But on actual inspection, no one will be found to have really returned to the house. Nonetheless, the very same sounds will be repeated a short time later in reality when the spouse does in fact return home. The first set of sounds are believed to have been made by the "forerunner" or *Vardogr* of the returning spouse. This invisible, sound-making forerunner would be similar to the "future" Goethe which the present Goethe glimpsed in a vision.

## The Animal as Prophet

Another side of prophecy is the animal as prophet. In his 1981 book *Psi Trek*, sociologist Laile E. Bartlett reports a discovery by Ruth Simon, a scientist with the U.S. Geological Survey, that roaches alter their behavior before an earthquake. The Japanese, for that matter, keep goldfish to warn them of impending quakes. When the fish start swimming frantically, their owners run outdoors in anticipation of a quake that might bring down or damage their building. The Soviets have gone so far as to set up animal quake-warning systems in their central Asian republic of Uzbekistan. Author Martin Ebon cites the case of thousands of water birds suddenly fleeing Montana's calm Lake Hegben on Aug. 17, 1959. Hours later, a series of earthquakes began, cracking the Hegben Dam, flooding and killing area residents as well as tourists in nearby Yellowstone Park. The birds, of course, were safe, and federal officials reported that rangers found no animal carcasses in the earthquake zone. Were the animals in the above cases psychically receiving information or just sensing faint tremors?

In a different precognitive example of "An Psi" (Animal psychic ability), a pet cocker spaniel named Merry was credited during World War II with saving the life of the Baines family of Wimbledon, a London suburb, by inspiring its masters to switch bomb shelters. Early in the war, Merry's owners had used an outside underground shelter for sleeping in case of bombing attacks. But for four years, that shelter had been abandoned in favor of a much less secure, in-house steel shelter under a table. Then, one day, a particular bombing attack blew out the windows of the Baines home, and Merry disappeared 12 hours later. The dog was eventually found to have broken into the family's long abandoned, boarded-up underground shelter. Four times, the dog was extracted, and the shelter reshuttered. Four times, Merry forced her way back inside and was always found sleeping on a bunk she had once shared with the Baines' daughter Audrey. Although the family had deserted the underground shelter in 1941 because of dampness, the Baineses experienced a "strange feeling" of security inside it. They decided to take the dog's lead and use the underground shelter again each night despite its dampness and stench. "As soon as we began to take an interest in the place (the new shelter), Merry left and spent the rest of the day about his own pursuits," Audrey Baines was quoted as saying. That night, a flying bomb destroyed the Baines home and several others in their Melbury Gardens neighborhood. But the Baineses were safely asleep in their underground shelter. Andrew MacKenzie recounted the Baines' story in his book *Riddle of the Future* after speaking with Audrey Baines and confirming the account with persons living in the area at the time.

## Futurists: Projectors of Trends

Another branch of prophecy includes the futurists. Unlike their metaphysical brethren, the futurists are scientists rather than psychics. They use logic to extrapolate current trends into the future. They also rationally analyze how present possibilities might develop. Three hundred years before the telephone, for example, the scientist and philosopher Sir Francis Bacon predicted that the future investigation of the physics of sound would one day enable it to be conveyed "over great distance through tubes."

Today, many futurists are on the payrolls of professional thinktanks, funded by corporations to guess the future. Unlike psychic prophets, the futurists often are much rosier in their assessments. For his part, futurist Herman Kahn, heading the Hudson Institute thinktank, predicted in a 1975 book that the planet's population will be generally affluent by 2100 due to a decreasing global birth rate, although he warned of greater instability in the near-term.

Futurists are also known for their imaginative forecasts of how growing technology might be used. A Rand Corporation physicist, for instance, conceived a 14,000 mile-per-hour mass transportation express system called Planetran that could shuttle passengers from New York City to Los Angeles in 54 minutes. The system would have floating "rocket" cars, electromagnetically moved through subterranean tunnels.

Meanwhile, in his 1982 bestseller *Megatrends*, the celebrated trend-mapper John Naisbitt cited 10 global tendencies already radically transforming our planet's future. They include:
* The shift from industrial-manufacturing societies to ones where information and ideas are the new commodities.
* The merging of national economies into a global economy.

77

* The crumbling of the hierarchical pyramid structure, as the pecking order gives way to informal networking among peers.
* Our previously either-or society with its narrow personal choices is now "exploding into a free-wheeling, multiple-option society," as Naisbett puts it.
* Other trends include the shift from north to south, from representative to participatory democracy, and decentralization.

## Orwell: A Literary "Futurist"

The logical projection of present trends into the future has its literary side. One of the most chilling instances of an author's projection is George Orwell's *1984*, the terrifying novel of a future totalitarian world. Orwell, a discouraged socialist had become alarmed over the threat posed to individual liberty by the rising fascist and Stalinist movements of the 20th Century. Orwell wrote his dark masterpiece in the late 1940s after, thanks to fascism, World War II had broken out and reduced much of the world to rubble. In Orwell's nightmare world, three brutal Stalinist police states minutely supervise every thought and action of their subjects throughout the earth. They constantly fight limited wars whose real purpose is just to keep industrial production going in their broken-down, poverty-line socialist economies. Party propagandists constantly rewrite history to keep it in accord with whatever political wind is blowing at the moment. Scientists, among others, practice "doublethink," the ability of a dogmatic person to hold contradictory beliefs simultaneously. For example, the Party scientist truly convinces himself that the earth, as the Party line dictates, is the center of the solar system. But he simultaneously conducts his lab work as if the sun is the center, so that experiments come out right. (Doublethink has already become a regular feature of political propaganda and corporate public relations.) On other fronts, "thought police" round up the few remaining dissidents for torture in the so-called Ministry of Love. The dissidents are brainwashed into loving the dictator, Big Brother. The dissidents then await the never-revealed day of their final execution. Orwell, whose real name was Eric Blair, died well before world totalitarianism apparently crested in the 1970s. Fortunately, totalitarianism today may well be receding with the rise of Third World democracies and the liberalization of much of the Communist bloc.

A completely different projected future was created by the British novelist Aldous Huxley, whose *Brave New World* looked 600 years ahead of the present. In the Brave New World, the growing chaos of an increasingly industrialized and technological world (world wars, strikes, etc.) are solved in a "positive" way. A benevolent ruling oligarchy uses bioengineering to slightly or greatly retard most humans mentally. The rulers allow only a small fraction of the population to attain full mental potential and become "alphas." Intense social conditioning, including subliminal sleep messages, also helps keep this caste system's behavior orderly and cooperative, as does a universally distributed drug and general affluence. Babies are born in test-tubes. Families are obsolete, and natural motherhood is considered obscene and socially disruptive. In this negative utopia, one of the 10 World Controllers explains how the benevolent dictatorship keeps everyone in a sick state of imagined happiness. "The world's stable now. People are happy; they get what they want, and they never want what they can't get," the world controller states. Again, like Orwell, Huxley wrote early in this turbulent century and did not live to see more favorable stabilizing trends, such as the recent beginnings of a collective social consciousness among individuals worldwide.

# Prophets of Doom

Still another face of prophecy is the perennial prophet of doom. One of the earliest prophets of doom was Cassandra, the princess of Bronze Age Troy, located in what is now Turkey. In Greek mythology, Cassandra was loved by Apollo, the handsome and amorous god of intellect and prophecy. Apollo even gave her the gift of prophecy. But Cassandra spurned Apollo's advances. Although angered, Apollo was helpless to take back his prophetic gift. Nevertheless, he avenged himself by decreeing that Cassandra would repeatedly foresee future disaster but her warnings would never be believed. So, during the fabled Trojan War between Troy and an alliance of Greek city states, Cassandra prophesied one coming tragedy after another, all to no avail. She even warned the Trojans not to bring the wooden "Trojan Horse," built by the Greeks and containing hidden Greek soldiers, inside Troy's defensive walls.

History is run through with this mythical theme of the doomsayer who is ignored or ridiculed but sees all the grim precognitions later fulfilled, step by step. No story better illustrates this than the tale of Jacques Cazotte. In 1788, Cazotte supposedly spoiled a festive party of progressive Parisian intellectuals and nobles in a startling way. He allegedly prophesied in detail how almost every dinner guest, including himself, would meet death within six years. This, he said, would all come about during a violent French Revolution. Here is how events supposedly unfolded:

## Doomsayer Spoils Party

The Duchess de Gramont gave a sumptuous dinner party and invited Paris' top conversationalists and wits. The liberal revelers enthusiastically discussed how a political revolution would soon sweep away France's corrupt aristocracy. In its place, intellectuals would usher in a benevolent golden age where reason ruled, the party-goers agreed. Already, the new thinking was everywhere among the people! At that point, an elderly mystic poet, Jacques Cazotte, perhaps annoyed, interrupted all the heady talk of benign revolution and enlightened rule. Cazotte said the eagerly sought revolution would indeed come soon, would indeed claim itself to be based on reason, but would instead be a bloodthirsty era, when not even women would be safe from execution and the king himself would be murdered. As for the guests' fates, Cazotte told the famous dramatist Sebastien Champfort that he would cut his veins 22 times with a razor but nonetheless would not die until some months afterward. Cazotte told the Marquis de Condorcet that he would poison himself in a prison cell to cheat his executioner. Turning to the noted astronomer Jean Bailly, Cazotte said Bailly would be guillotined along with guests Jean Roucher and Monsieur de Nicolai. Cazotte told his personal enemy, the die-hard atheist Jean-Francois de La Harpe, that La Harpe would be spared and would convert to Catholicism. That remark touched off uproarious laughter among the skeptical party revelers. "Ah, now I feel reassured," Champfort wise-cracked. "If we are not to perish until La Harpe becomes a Christian, we are practically immortal." Eventually, Cazotte indirectly predicted his own doom.

La Harpe wrote down the evening's prophecies in his diary, hoping to disgrace Cazotte later with their falsity. But a year after the party, the French Revolution indeed broke out. Starting with lofty idealism, it soon degenerated into a brutal Reign of Terror. In 1794, the Marquis de Condorcet poisoned himself in prison to escape the guillotine, as Cazotte had foreseen. In 1793, Champfort cut his wrists 22 times, assuming his arrest was imminent. But he actually died two months later as a result of poor medical treatment of the injuries, just as Cazotte had said. Cazotte was also right about Bailley, Roucher and de Nicolai, whose heads rolled from the guillotine. As for La Harpe, he was thrown into a dungeon, where he experienced an ardent religious conversion to Catholicism. La Harpe survived the Reign of Terror and joined a monastery. Cazotte was right again. Indeed, the Duchess de Gramont and other ladies at the party were also executed, as were King Louis XVI and his queen, Marie Antoinette. During the revolution, Cazotte told friends there was no cause to celebrate his release after an arrest. There would be another, fatal arrest later, he said. It came in 1792, when Cazotte was guillotined as a counter-revolutionary. The seer had been wrong, though, about dinner guest Felix Vicq-d'Azur, who died of a fever rather than as a prison suicide, as Cazotte had said he would.

An amazing story. But is it true? On the one hand, a written record of Cazotte's supposed prophecy was not discovered until after the French Revolution had run its course. After La Harpe's death in post-revolutionary 1803, the records of Cazotte's prophecy were discovered among La Harpe's documents. Nevertheless, the turn-of-the-century parapsychologist, Walter Bormann, did find bolstering evidence for a pre-revolution prophecy from many sources. Among other things, Borman turned up a letter written in 1825 by the Countess de Genlis to a Dr. Deleuze in which she wrote: "A hundred times before the Revolution, I heard M. de La Harpe tell it (Cazotte's prophecy), and always almost exactly as it had been printed..." As another example, other witnesses said the celebrated Vicq-d'Azur had been quite disturbed by Cazotte's descriptions, though remaining skeptical.

# A Condemned Man's Prophecy

Another prophecy of doom, uttered by the Highland Scots seer, Coinneach Odhar, required two centuries for its step-by-step fulfillment. In the 1600s, just before his grisly execution at the hands of Countess Isabella of Seaforth, a vengeful Odhar prophesied a tragic end for Isabella's noble family of Seaforth. Generations of Scots then waited for Odhar's detailed predictions to be realized.

Trouble between Odhar and the countess had begun after she had summoned him to the Seaforth castle on an urgent mission. The worried countess wanted Odhar to look into his scrying stone and see whether her husband, the earl of Seaforth, was safe. The earl had been away in France on business for an extended period but had not sent her any word of himself. Looking into his stone, Odhar laughed with gusto at his psychic vision of the earl and assured the countess she need not fear for her lord. But the seer refused to elaborate on what he saw. However, when the countess threatened him, Odhar revealed that he had seen the earl in a luxurious room in Paris, with an arm around a beautiful woman, whose hand he was kissing. Shamed before her company, the countess flew into a rage and ordered that Odhar be burned alive. According to one version of the Odhar story, the seer made his condemning prophecy about the Seaforth family shortly before he was pushed headfirst into a barrel of boiling tar. "I see into the far future," Odhar said, "and I read the doom of the race of my oppressor, and die mourning." Odhar went on to say that the historic Seaforth family would die out after a few more generations. The last earl of Seaforth would be both deaf and dumb and would see all four of his sons die before he himself passed on. After the last earl's death, the "remnant" of his estate would be inherited by a "white-hooded lassie from the East, and she shall kill her sister," Odhar predicted. The last earl would know he is the prophesied one because his aristocratic neighbors from the estates of Gairloch, Chisholm, Grant and Ramsey would be buck-toothed, hair-lipped, half-witted and a stammerer, Odhar remarked.

In 1754, the prophecy apparently began to come true with the birth of Francis Humberston Mackenzie, who, in 1797, became the earl of Seaforth. Three decades earlier, at around age 12, Mackenzie had become deaf because of a bout with scarlet fever. Mackenzie had four sons, and all died before their time. Before Mackenzie died in 1815 as the last earl of Seaforth, following all his sons to the grave, he lost his speech. Of four neighboring landlords of Mackenzie's, one turned out to be buck-toothed, another harelipped, another half-witted, and another a stammerer. As for Odhar's "white-hooded lassie from the east" -- Mackenzie's recently widowed daughter, Mary MacKenzie Hood, wearing a traditional white garb of mourning, returned to Scotland from India to claim the dwindling Seaforth holdings. Sales of estate lands were following one upon another, unremittingly, for various reasons. The multiple tragedies climaxed when Lady Hood was driving her sister Caroline in a carriage that overturned when its ponies spooked, mortally wounding the sister, as Odhar had foreseen. Odhar's alleged vision had been consummated in every detail.

In 1878, Duncan Davidson, the lord lieutenant of Ross, commented in a letter: "Many of these prophecies I heard upwards of seventy years ago, and when many of them were not yet fulfilled, such as Lord Seaforth surviving his sons, and (Lady Hood)'s accident near Brahan, by which Miss Caroline Mackenzie was killed."

## Tabloid Seers: Often Wrong

In this era of popularization, prophecy has been no exception. Periodically, the supermarket racks are stuffed with tabloid front pages featuring double-decker rows of mugshots of select psychics, offering predictions to interest the masses. These prognostications are often colorful, sometimes catastrophic, but nearly always dead wrong.

*The Book of Predictions* checked 360 predictions by 10 psychics published in the *National Enquirer* between 1976 and 1979 and determined that four psychics each got one forecast right. Six got nothing right. In all, the seers were 99 percent off the mark. Even the successful predictions were generally lackluster. "The big names have become famous scoring a few dramatic hits, but at times, they've all been very wrong," wrote Joe Fisher and his collaborator Peter Commins in their book *Predictions*. "We remember the successes and tend to forget the failures, perhaps because we have a need to believe."

One reason the tabloid seers so often go wrong may have to do with the kind of predictions they many times are making: Generalized, sweeping pronouncements about wars, gigantic upheavals and the like. Such prophecies, some observers say, frequently go wrong because there is no close, emotional connection between the psychic and his predicted event. Strong emotion or personal involvement seems many times to be a key to facilitating the accuracy and vividness of a prophecy.

## Croesus and Delphic Prophecy

Prophecy also has a very ancient face. In ancient times, the map was dotted with religious shrines where pilgrims went to ask for prophetic counsel from priests who claimed to act as human mediums, speaking for gods. The most famous such shrine was on a mountainside at the Greek town of Delphi, just north of Athens. For a thousand years, the shrine at Delphi was a Mecca for kings and aristocrats of the ancient world, who trekked there with questions about the future. At Delphi, a priestess, speaking for the god of prophecy Apollo, sat on a tripod. According to legend, she supposedly inhaled intoxicating fumes rising from a crevice, which inspired her prophecies.

Typical of the powerful pilgrims to Delphi was the fabulously wealthy King of Lydia, Croesus, who arrived at the shrine in the 500s B.C. Croesus was concerned about the growing power of the Persian Empire on his border and was considering an attack on the Persians. Therefore, Croesus asked the priestess about the outcome of a possible war between Lydia and Persia. The priestess replied: "After crossing the Halys (River -- the boundary between Lydia and the Persian Empire), Croesus will destroy a great empire." Croesus had gratefully gifted the Delphic shrine with a 570-pound gold lion and other lavish valuables before marching off against the Persians. But it turned out to be Croesus' great army that the priestess was referring to.

84

Centuries later, the delphic shrine received another notable visitor. This time, it was the brutal, insane Roman emperor Nero, who used Christians as living torches to light his nighttime spectacles and murdered his mother Agrippina in 59 A.D. to please his mistress, among numerous other atrocities. Nero's visit to the shrine came shortly after his mother's death. "Your presence outrages the god you seek," the priestess shouted at Nero. "Go back, matricide. The number 73 marks the hour of your downfall." Nero, then 30, was not worried about losing power at age 73, so far off. In his characteristic style, he avenged himself by ordering that the hands and feet of the shrine's priests be cut off. Nero then ordered that the priests and their priestess be buried alive. Unfortunately for the tyrant Nero, only a few years later, in 67 A.D., he was overthrown after a military mutiny and committed suicide. The number 73 turned out to refer not to Nero's age at his downfall but to the age of his successor, the elderly Galba.

The delphic shrine gradually lost influence over several centuries, and with the rise of Christianity, the pilgrimages ceased altogether. Today, modern researchers will never know if true prophecy occurred at the opulently wealthy shrine. But the ancient Roman orator Cicero did have a point when he noted: "Never could the oracle of Delphi have been so overwhelmed with so many important offerings from monarchs and nations if all the ages had not proved the truth of its oracles."

# Biblical Prophecy

In the Western world, prophecy's most familiar face is Biblical. The long roots of Bible prophecy go back to the ancient Hebrew *nabhi* ("called persons") -- wandering flute, harp or tambourine players who went into fits of ecstasy when "breathed upon" by God's spirit. During these ecstasies, the nabhi leaped around, sang, saw visions and prophesied.

Later came the familiar Old Testament prophets, who usually predicted some doom awaiting Israel for having sinned against Yahweh, the Hebrew god. For example, in the 700s B.C., the prophet Amos, a simple shepherd, decried the nobility's exploitation of the poor and the people's apathy toward God. Amos forecast the annihilation of the northern Jewish kingdom of Israel. In the 700s B.C., the Assyrian Empire, the Nazi Germany of the ancient world, indeed destroyed Israel and carried off the famous Ten Lost Tribes in a mass deportation designed to prevent future rebellion. The southern Jewish kingdom of Judah, with its remaining two Hebrew tribes, survived. But around a century later, Judah herself had fallen into idolatry and sin. The prophet Jeremiah dramatized his prophecy of Judah's coming doom at the hands of the Babylonian Empire by walking around Jerusalem with a yoke of captivity over his shoulders. For his efforts, the skeptical had him thrown into a pit and a dungeon. Yet, later, as the Babylonians were about to invade Jerusalem, the vindicated Jeremiah bought a piece of land to dramatize his prophecy that the doomed city would one day be restored. Meanwhile, the prophet Micah, a peasant farmer, foresaw a future time of worldwide peace when all humanity would worship one God. "What does the Lord require of you, but to act justly, to love mercy and to walk humbly with your God?" Micah declared with touching eloquence.

A major Biblical theme -- mentioned 300 times -- is the predicted coming of a Messiah (an "anointed one") to liberate the Jewish race. Some Bible prophecies said the Messiah would be a revolutionary political liberator, helping Israel fight itself free of foreign imperialists. Other prophecies said the Messiah would, instead, be a meek, "suffering servant" leading his people on an inward spiritual path of liberation. Christianity argues that Christ fulfilled the prophecy of the "suffering servant." Judaism argues that the Messiah has not yet come.

According to the New Testament gospel writers, Christ could foresee the future and had other miraculous powers, which included healing and telepathy. In the gospels, Christ repeatedly predicts the manner of his coming death and resurrection, foresees the destruction of the Jewish temple by the Romans, and predicts that his leading disciple, Simon Peter, will fearfully deny to others that he has been connected with the outlawed and arrested Jesus.

In the Western world, prophecy's most familiar face is Biblical.
Here, the Old Testament prophet Elijah is nourished by an angel, a
Gustave Dore illustration of the legendary story in the first Book of
Kings.

Jesus of Nazareth frequently displayed prophetic powers, according to the New Testament writers. Above, Jesus shares the Last Supper with his disciples, just before his arrest. It was there that he warned them that one of the Twelve would betray him.

For centuries, the religious shrine of the Greek god Apollo at Delphi, Greece, attracted kings and aristocrats from all over the ancient world. Shown above are Apollo, the god of prophecy, and his twin sister, Artemis, the goddess of the moon.

# Astrology

From the dawn of civilization until the 1600s, astrology enjoyed a matter-of-fact, near-universal acceptance around the world. Then, that acceptance began to turn to near-universal scorn among the well educated in the Western world. In any case, it was not until this century that astrology's claims were ever subjected to rigorous scientific scrutiny. Perhaps not surprisingly, the tantalizing truth which has emerged seems to lie in between the two extremes of blind credulity and kneejerk rejection, as we will soon see.

The idea that heavenly bodies can be watched to foretell the future goes back at least 5,000 years to the Middle Eastern farming city states of Sumer, the world's first civilization. In fact, the Old Testament's legendary story of the Tower of Babel is thought to be based on the huge Babylonian towers which ancient Mesopotamian astrologers climbed to get a good look at the heavens. Over the thousands of years, astrology has so permeated our thinking that the world's languages are now peppered with its terms, including the English words lunacy (crazed by the moon), ill-starred, disastrous (against the stars), saturnine (gloomy and grave, from the influence of Saturn) and jovial (genial and merry, from the influence of Jupiter).

## Astrology's Tool: the Horoscope

Astrology's tool in predicting the future is a chart called a horoscope (from Greek *skopein*, to view, and *hora*, hour of birth), and the best known type of horoscope is the birth chart. The birth chart shows the sky positions of heavenly bodies and key zodiac constellations at the moment a person is born. Two of the most powerful and telling influences in a person's birth chart are supposedly the position of the sun and also the zodiac constellation that happens to be rising in the east, both of which govern an individual's personality type. (For example, if the sun is in the constellation Libra the Scales at birth, astrologers consider the person a "Libran," supposedly tending to be a fair-minded mediator, such as a judge.) Complicating this picture even more are the planets. They have their own refining influences on the basic portrait of a person painted by the sun and the rising sign. Jupiter, for example, supposedly can foreshadow expansiveness, generosity and similar traits, but Saturn's influence is restrictive and can portend such specifics as hardship or a well-disciplined nature. How the planets influence a person also depends on which zodiac constellations they happen to be in. For each of these zodiac constellations has its own traits. For example, the constellation Leo symbolizes confidence and authoritativeness while Gemini symbolizes the articulate communicator. The planetary influences can also help or harm, depending on the good or bad angles which the planets are forming with each other in the sky.

To say the least, astrology has had its ups and downs over the past five millennia. In Sumerian and later Babylonian times, horoscopes were routinely cast merely to see the future course of the nation, not the individual, which was a later idea. During the late Roman Empire of the 300s A.D., astrology was in decline and virtually finished off by the new Christian faith. Mohammedism, however, rapidly expanding in Africa and the Near East in the 600s and 700s A.D., embraced and nurtured astrology, later reintroducing it to Europe in the Middle Ages. Astrology then spread through Europe with enthusiasm, the Christian Church itself unofficially accepted it, and several popes became astrologers. By the 1500s, Europeans considered astrology to be the noble "queen of the sciences." But the scientific revolution of the 1600s brought to light a sun-centered, not earth-centered, solar system as well as other discoveries at odds with traditional astrological thinking. Modern scientific astronomy split off from astrology at that point, and astrology was again on a downhill run, this decline lasting until the 20th Century. Then, a gradual rebirth of astrological interest suddenly skyrocketed in the iconoclastic 1960s, especially among the highly educated young. By 1978, 40 percent of Americans aged 13 to 18 thought astrology was valid, according to a Gallup Poll; 55 percent by 1984. The story of astrology's renaissance climaxed in the spring of 1988 when it became known that none other than First Lady Nancy Reagan at times ordered the President's schedule altered because of astrological portents. Mrs. Reagan, it turned out, had turned to astrology in 1981 to help protect the President after Reagan had nearly died in an assassination attempt. From then on, certain presidential schedulings were checked out astrologically ahead of time by Mrs. Reagan's astrologer, Joan Quigley of San Francisco. By 1988, astrology had become so accepted by the general public that the sensational revelation of astrological presidential scheduling turned out not to be a political disaster for President Reagan but a boon to astrologers. Today, there are more than 10,000 professional astrologers in the U.S., some involved in such narrow specialities as real estate transactions and stock market forecasting. Numerous daily newspapers have astrology forecast columns, though many astrologers consider them inaccurate because they ignore all factors except sun signs and are supposedly far too overgeneralized. Astrology, incidentally, never lost its standing in the orient while it was in eclipse, so to speak, in the West. No less an occasion than the granting of independence by Britain to India in 1947 was moved up by one day to achieve better timing astrologically.

## Criticisms of Astrology

Astrology's huge public following today in West and East, however does not necessarily validate it. As Jean De La Bruyere put it in the 1600s, "The exact contrary of what is generally believed is often the truth." In fact, skeptics have been ferocious in their attacks on astrology, perhaps out of desperation as it gains more and more followers. As early as Roman times, the historic orator Cicero denounced astrology as an "incredible mad folly which is daily refuted by experience." A chief criticism of astrology is that astrologers are not even united in using the same system! Because of a slow wobbling of the earth on its axis as it rotates around daily and orbits about the sun yearly, the zodiac signs now cover different sky territory than they did 2,000 years ago. For example, a person born under one zodiac sign two millennia ago, would be born under a completely different one today. This should have drastic astrological consequences, since neighboring zodiac signs have quite different traits. Some astrologers, the skeptics point out, have adjusted their calculations for this wobbling but others decline to do so. On another front, astrologers, the skeptics note, are not all agreed on whether the recently discovered outer planets should be used in astrological calculations along with the six planets known since ancient times. Critics also scoff at claimed spectacular astrological predictions. Sir Francis Bacon, a pioneer of modern science, said three centuries ago: "Men mark when they hit and never mark when they miss," although the great ancient astronomer Ptolemy countered: "We do not discredit the art of the navigator for its many errors."

Typical of claimed astrological "hits" was the Persian astrologer-poet Anwari's prediction of an international cataclysm for Sept. 16, 1186. Anwari noted that the sun, moon, Saturn, Jupiter and Mars would all be huddled close together that night in the constellation Libra the Scales. But nothing happened when that date rolled around. Later, though, astrologers claimed that Anwari's cataclysm had indeed occurred, after all, but in an unexpected fashion. On the night of Sept. 16, a Mongol child named Temujin was born, who later organized the wild and fierce Mongol barbarians for a lightning and terrifying conquest and sacking of Asia in the early 1200s. In 1208, Temujin was given the name Genghis Khan (Chinese *cheng-sze*, "precious warrior"; Turkish *khan*, "lord.")

## Astrology Gets Statistical Support

Despite astrology's unscientific origins and glaring inconsistencies, modern researchers may be at least partly verifying the ancient practice. The most striking research, which has supported some claims of astrology but cast doubt on others, was conducted for more than 20 years by the French psychologist Michel Gauquelin and his then-wife Francoise. In one study with anti-astrological results, Gauquelin checked the horoscopes of 600 French convicted murderers and could find no astrological indicators whatever of their unhappy situation. On another front, Gauquelin went on to statistically debunk various astrological ideas, such as the notion that Saturn and Mars are often near a dying person's sun sign.

But on the positive side, Gauquelin's rigorous research did uncover a clear statistical link between the celestial positions of planets and success in certain professions. In the mid-1950s, Gauquelin collected more than 25,000 birth records of mostly prominent individuals from five European countries. Out of more than 3,000 doctors and scientists examined, Gauquelin found that Mars was just rising above the horizon or was directly overhead at birth in so many cases that the results beat odds of 500,000 to 1. A just rising or directly overhead Mars also dominated in a large sampling of sports champions, a result that beat odds of 5 million to one. Significantly, the Mars archetype has traditionally been associated with undertakings of major energy, persistence, and stamina, such as athletics and soldiering, among other things.

Gauquelin turned up other statistically important findings with outstanding writers, politicians, soldiers and journalists. For example, politicians tended to be born when Jupiter was rising above the horizon, while long-distance runners and others working alone had a stronger connection with the moon than with any planet.

In 1968, Gauquelin's Mars effect results with sports champions were reproduced independently by a group of Belgian scientists, much to their surprise. Also, three prominent statisticians retraced Gauquelin's methods and computations and found no flaws in them. Although others have attacked Gauquelin's methodology, his research generally has appeared to stand up to scrutiny.

Intriguingly, no correlations were found between planetary positions and professions except where the subjects were notably successful in their fields. In fact, an independent 1986 follow-up look at Gauquelin's sports champions by University of Gottingen Professor Suitbert Ertel showed that the Mars effect steadily increased as the distinction of the notable sports champions did.

Gauquelin's study, incidentally, had another twist. The presence of a planet might **hinder** a profession. Gauquelin could find no celebrated French writer who had Saturn rising at the time of his birth, and artists were rarely born when Mars was moving over the horizon.

Gauquelin's 25,000-record survey did not yield any significant statistical relationships for the sun, Mercury, Venus, Uranus, Neptune, Pluto, or the signs of the zodiac. And some of the astrological relationships he did find did not match traditional astrological thinking.

## Jung Studies Marital Horoscopes

The great Swiss psychiatrist Carl Jung, who popularized the idea of the collective unconscious, also experimented with astrology. Jung analyzed the horoscopes of 483 randomly chosen married couples, looking for any notable astrological relationships. Jung also checked a control group of unmarried people, consisting of 32,000 pairs of charts. In the end, Jung concluded that he had found several astrological relationships in his experimental group, but none in the control group. In particular, the position of the moon at a wife's birth tended to be very close to the position of either the sun, moon or rising sign at her husband's birth. (The rising sign is the zodiac constellation just rising in the east at the moment of birth.) The odds of obtaining Jung's statistically significant results by chance alone are 1 in 10,000.

In 1959, psychologist Vernon Clark decided to test an astrologer's ability to make predictions about people from unidentified birth charts. Clark gathered 10 horoscopes from a smorgasbord of professions ranging from puppeteer to reptile specialist. He gave the birth charts to an experimental group of 20 astrologers and also to a control group of 20 social workers or psychologists. Each of the groups received a list of professions and was told to match the profession with the appropriate horoscope. The control group performed no better than chance. But 17 of the 20 astrologers had a matchup success rate that would have required 100 to 1 odds to be due to chance alone.

In a second experiment, Clark distributed 10 pairs of horoscopes to the same astrologers. Attached to each pair of charts was a list of key life events pertaining to only one of the two people for whom the charts had been prepared. Each astrologer was challenged to decide which life event list corresponded to which horoscope. In the end, three astrologers had perfect scores. The others' performance achieved odds of better than 100 to 1 against chance. However, studies similar to Clark's have also yielded poor performances by astrologers. What's more, some observers have wondered whether it might be precognition and clairvoyance, rather than astrological signs, that are actually responsible for some astrological successes.

## Magnetic Storms & Moon Madness

In the early 1950s, the American electronic engineer John H. Nelson drew attention to the fact that earthly magnetic storms, which disrupt radio reception, are linked to planetary positions. The storms occur when nearby planets, as seen from earth, form 90-degree and 180-degree angles. These angles, strangely, correspond to unfavorable planetary angles in astrology, as opposed to such favorable angles as 60 degrees apart or 120 degrees. Indeed, Nelson later discovered that when nearby planets were 60 and 120 degrees apart, magnetic disturbances were not present here and short-wave reception was good. Using his theory, Nelson achieved a 93 percent accuracy rate in predicting magnetic disturbances.

Still more evidence of some sort of link between the heavens and the earth comes from the phenomenon of moon madness. In fact, moon-induced madness is, strictly speaking, the meaning of the word "lunacy," whose root is linked to the Latin word for the moon, *luna*.

In his book *Supernature*, Lyall Watson notes: "Superintendents of asylums have always feared the influence of the moon on 'loony' inmates and canceled staff leaves on nights when the moon is full." Watson also cited a report by the American Institute of Medical Climatology linking the full moon with peaking incidents of psychotic crimes like homicidal alcoholism. In the 1700s, English law distinguished lunatic behavior -- that is moon-induced madness -- from ordinary insanity. The lunatic received more leniency for his crimes than the ordinary insane person.

## Theories of How Astrology Works

If at least some of astrology's tenets could possibly be valid, how would heavenly bodies actually work their effects on us? One of two leading theories about this, the "causative" theory, holds that that heavenly objects send out controlling emanations of some sort, like subtle radiations. But today, this out-of-favor hypothesis has been overshadowed by the synchronistic theory. This idea holds that everything in the universe is somehow connected to everything else. The movements of the stars and heavenly bodies are simply synchronized with developments on earth. When something happens in the sky, there is a corresponding thing happening synchronously on earth. Neither causes the other.

In the book *Cosmic Connections*, astrologer Caroline Casey is quoted discussing the stimulating zodiac sign of beginnings, Aries: "Astrology is a language of correlation. It says, for instance: There is an energy out there that we'll call Aries, which we also see in things that are bright red, and that describes things that start and describes springtime and red berries and the spice cinnamon and stimulants. This language ties a lot of things together and says, here's how you can see this thing that we're talking about in different forms. There are herbs that are Aries. Springtime is the season. Red is the color. C-natural is the musical note." Casey thus describes various things that either mark the beginning of something, like a musical scale, or stimulate, like the color red, the color of revolution, among other things. Red also is the "beginning" color of the visible spectrum. She goes on: "Astrology tracks the hidden relationship between things that are not obviously related on surface inspection. It's a language that says there is a harmony and correlation that runs through all of creation."

This sounds much like the idea which philosophers call the *law of correspondence*. It is the idea that **a fundamental principle of reality** (such as the beginning of something, to use Ms. Casey's example) expresses itself throughout wildly different areas of nature in **corresponding forms**. Attractive gravity in physics and the attracting emotion of love, for example, have often been compared. Understood in this light, one might consider the planets to be symbols of major principles or archetypes. A certain mix of planetary positions might signal, at a given moment such as a person's time of birth, a corresponding mix of similar principles active on earth in an individual or nation.

# A Jungle of Divination Methods

Whatever the truth of astrology, it is just one of literally thousands of so-called *divination* systems. Divination is the art of supernaturally getting hidden information. That information is often about the future but not always. For example, diviners called dowsers claim they can find underground water. And divination once was used to decide the guilt or innocence of someone accused of a crime, a process called an *ordeal*. For instance, in European and colonial American witchcraft trials of the 1600s, an accused witch was often bound with rope and pitched into water. If the defendant sank, he was considered innocent. But if he floated, he was regarded as a witch and put to death. An early no-win situation.

Still, the emphasis in divination is on glimpsing the future. Some divination systems, like astrology, interpret symbolic happenings in the outside world (symbolic star and planet patterns, in astrology's case) to understand how earthly events will unfold. In other cases, such as crystal ball gazing and tea leaf reading, the diviner may simply use the technique to sharpen his concentration so that he can clairvoyantly obtain psychic information.

Some of history's most famous "diviners" were the ancient roman priests known as *augurs*. They checked the behavior of animals and even inspected their intestines (the art of *haruspicy*) in search of omens about the future. These priests enjoyed immense authority since no major events, not even declarations of war or elections, would occur without their agreeing that the omens for success were good. Other widely popular divining methods through the ages have included card reading, numerology and palmistry. Some believe that card reading and similar techniques rely on synchronicity to make the correct answer come up in response to a question.

Besides the familiar divining techniques, there are hundreds, perhaps thousands, of little-known and often quite bizarre methods. The names of most of these methods end in the suffix "-mancy" from the Greek *manteia*, meaning "divination." The techniques include:

* Cephalomancy. Boiling an ass' head among coals. It was thought that the jaws would move at the mention of a guilty person's name.

* Myomancy. Divining the future by interpreting the sounds of and the damage done by mice. The Roman dictator Fabius Maximus stepped down from power after believing himself to be warned by the squeal of a mouse.

* Omphalomancy. Studying your navel to divine the future.

* Ovomancy. Noting which shapes form when egg whites are dropped into water.

* Daphnomancy. Attending to the sound which laurel leaves make, if any, when cast onto a fire. This idea may go back to the sudden withering of a grove of laurel trees in the ancient city of Rome during the last year of life of the Emperor Nero. Nero's death marked the end of the Caesarian dynasty, and the death of the grove was considered a foretokening omen of the dynasty's end. That was because, for decades, more and more laurel trees had been planted in the grove each time a different Caesar had become emperor.

* Tyromancy. Observing the curdling of cheese.

* Onomancy. Checking the letters of a person's name to divine his fortune.

* Gelomancy. Analyzing wild laughter.

## Idi Amin's Prophetic Turtle

The above methods just scratch the surface of techniques, some of them credulity-straining, to say the least. Still another divination art crops up in a possibly true story originating in the days when the brutal dictator Idi Amin enforced a reign of terror in the African nation of Uganda. Supposedly, a turtle used for telling fortunes predicted, correctly as it turned out later, the fall of the burly, erratic Amin. But the turtle did not last long enough to see its prophecy fulfilled, ending its days beforehand in a soup bowl as punishment.

Even postage stamps have shown themselves to be potential instruments of prophecy, according to an 1988 article in *Fate* magazine by George W. Earley. On May 14, 1918, stamp collector William T. Robey bought a sheet of 100 air mail stamps, part of the first such issue in this country. On each stamp was pictured a particular Curtiss JN4-H airplane, #38262 to be exact. Robey discovered, however, that his sheet of airplane stamps, because of a printing error, had each plane upside down. And this was the only sheet with that error. Robey soon sold the $24 sheet as a philatelic rarity for $15,000, big money in those days. Prophecy was the farthest thing from Robey's mind. But the day after Robey's purchase of the stamps at the post office, Lt. George Boyle took off in the same Curtiss JN4-H #38262 featured upside-down on Robey's sheet of stamps. Boyle was beginning America's first air mail flight. But Boyle flew in the wrong direction and eventually landed awkwardly. Boyle and his plane ended up upside-down, just as the plane was pictured on the 100 stamps which Robey had bought.

Considering how widely fortune-telling ranges in its methods and credibility, a warning by the leading psychic Eileen Garrett in her book *The Sense and Nonsense of Prophecy* is worth heeding: "Modern man, like his primitive ancestors, still pays homage to the soothsayer who can offer a reassuring word and a bright future. And I am afraid that that is about all that most crystal gazers can supply, whether that bright future is there or not... The lights are low, the price is high, the atmosphere is dim, and the future is bright. But that future depends on what you do and not on the dazzling crystal."

# History's Most Revered System

Perhaps the most revered divination system in history centers around a 5,000-year-old Chinese classic called the *Book of Changes* or *I Ching* (pronounced EE JING), one of the world's oldest books. The towering Chinese philosopher Confucius himself said, at age 69 in 481 B.C., that he would spend 50 more years studying the volume if he could live that long. The book contains 64 profound and symbolic essays with multiple layers of meaning, each describing a particular life condition or human trait. Usually, the inquirer of the *Book of Changes* meditates on a particular question or personal crisis while throwing a group of three coins six times. The results of these tosses are used in assembling a stick figure of six solid or broken lines, depending on how the coins come up as heads or tails. This stick figure is called a hexagram. The inquirer then reads the book essay which corresponds to the hexagram figure. The essays purportedly give insight into the life direction which the inquirer should be taking in connection with the question being meditated upon. In doing so, the essays advise the questioner on whether a particular life course should be followed, noting which actions a spiritually evolved "Superior Man" would take. The book mentions probable outcomes of various alternative courses of action. All this points up the fact that the *I Ching's* main purpose is not mere fortune-telling. The book, its proponents say, is actually a manual containing a whole system of philosophy to enlighten a sincere spiritual seeker.

The philosopher Jung experimented heavily with the *I Ching*. He concluded that synchronicity is at work in making sure that the inquirer's concerns are matched through the coin-toss selection process with the appropriate hexagram. Certainly, for centuries, experienced *I Ching* users have sworn by what they call the book's uncanny accuracy. These claims were put to a scientific test in the early 1970s by Lawrence Rubin and Charles Honorton at Brooklyn's Maimonides Medical Center. Rubin and Honorton had 40 persons ask questions and toss coins for *I Ching* responses. Each subject was then shown two hexagrams, the correct one and a false one which had been randomly selected. Those who had faith in the *I Ching* generally could identify the correct hexagram as a more appropriate answer. But skeptics generally could not distinguish between the real and bogus hexagrams.

Each hexagram and its essay deals with a different life condition represented by a particular mixture of "yin and yang." The yin and yang, according to the ancient religion of Taoism and the philosophy of Confucianism, are the universal forces of male energy and female energy, respectively. Taoists contend that everything in the universe can be fundamentally reduced to these two forces, which run through all things, opposing but also complementing each other. The male-female contrast is seen in such complementary oppositions as logic-intuition, strength-weakness, radiance-reflectivity, activity-passivity, sun-moon, creative-receptive, hard-yielding, leader-follower, day-night, and so on ad infinitum. According to this way of thinking, human beings, whether male or female, are a usually unbalanced mixture of the yin and yang energies within them. Even societies reflect this imbalance. The scientific and technological West has had a male or yang dominance for the last 300 years, while in the mystical and reflective East, the yin force has dominated. Better balancing of the yin and yang energies is thought to improve one's life.

Despite its loyal following, the *I Ching* is not without detractors. Critics say the essays are so vague and generalized that they can mean virtually anything to anybody. Detractors have also noted contradictory translations in use from the original Chinese. Nevertheless, the *I Ching* has had an enormous influence on far eastern culture for millennia. In fact, the modern flag of South Korea features an ancient symbol of the yin and yang surrounded by four *trigrams*. These are three-line halves of the six-line hexagrams. The trigrams symbolize life conditions of their own and are interpreted in conjunction with the hexagrams.

The Three Wise Men, astrologers from the east, are guided to
Jesus' birthplace by the Star of Bethlehem.

A striking woodcut from the 1500s depicts the different parts of a horoscope. The center of the horoscope is surrounded by concentric rings showing the planetary signs, the zodiac signs and the 12 astrological houses. Finally, heavenly forces are shown beyond the outermost ring.

Above: At age 69, the ancient Chinese philosopher Confucius said
he would spend 50 more years studying the I Ching if he could live
that long. Below: A Taoist image. The inner circle is divided between the white, masculine yang and the black, feminine yin, showing the eternal interplay of the two forces. Outside the circle are
eight trigrams.

# Nostradamus

Four hundred years ago, a courageous plague-fighting French physician and astrologer, Michel de Nostredame, better known as Nostradamus, allegedly displayed the greatest prophetic powers the modern world has seen. These powers supposedly became more noticeable as he wandered grief-stricken through France and Italy after disease had killed his young wife and two small sons. One legend claims that the journeying Nostradamus once suddenly knelt respectfully before a young, undistinguished friar, calling him, "His Holiness." Nineteen years after Nostradamus died, this onetime friar and ex-swineherd, Felix Peretti, was proclaimed Pope Sixtus V. After Nostradamus' wanderings ended, he eventually wrote a book containing 942 four-line rhymed verses. The verses purported to tell the future of the world from 1555 until 3797 A.D.

Since then, a Cold War has raged over Nostradamus' authenticity. On one side, Nostradamus believers have credited him, among other things, with a detailed prediction of the French Revolution and the rise of Napoleon, all a century and a half in the future. Some supporters have controversially asserted that Nostradamus even identified Napoleon and Hitler by name. A few Nostradamus zealots have ascribed virtually every modern happening, from air raids to AIDS, to one of his prophecies or another. On the other side are skeptics who say Nostradamus has pulled off a gigantic 400-year-old hoax to mock his contemporaries' ignorance and to build wealth and fame.

Fueling the shrill debate is the vagueness of Nostradamus' prophetic book, titled the *Centuries* because its prophecies are grouped in 100s. Nostradamus did commit himself by publishing his prophecies, starting in 1555, which is more than many prophets are willing to do. But he also heavily obscured those prophecies. In writing them, he used anagrams (word jumbles such as Ripas for Paris), puns, mythological references, symbolic language, obsolete place names, and foreign vocabulary for French words, among other devices. Nostradamus even scrambled the order in which the prophecies appear, so there is no chronological sequence. What resulted was an elaborate code which only mammoth scholarship and detective work could decipher. Indeed, to the uninitiated, a superficial look at the prophetic verses usually yields gibberish.

Nostradamus said he deliberately veiled his verses to keep from being accused of sorcery. Certainly, he probably also wanted to ensure that a negative prophecy about a powerful person or institution should not be too obvious, to protect himself against retaliation in a harsh age. Cynics have offered another motivation: By obscuring and often (though not always) generalizing the prophecies, Nostradamus permitted a vast number of later historical developments to be "read into" many of the cryptic verses. Thus, he made possible many (accidental) "hits." Yet the same vagueness makes it hard to say a prophecy was wrong.

## Nostradamus and Napoleon

Did Nostradamus foresee the hapless King Louis XVI, the violent French Revolution and its Reign of Terror, the rise of Napoleon's European empire and the dictator's final island exile? Some analysts have found what they believe to be frequent Nostradamian references to the Napoleonic era of the 1790s and early 1800s.

While commentators concede that other interpretations are certainly possible, some say the seer wrote of Napoleon when he prophesied: "An Emperor shall be born near Italy/ Who shall cost the Empire dear/ When it is seen with whom he allies himself/ He shall be found less a prince than a butcher." Napoleon was born on the island of Corsica off the Italian coast. Wielding military might as France's dictator, the so-called "Corsican Adventurer" forced other nations into alliances with France and helped plunge Europe into a series of devastating, continent-wide wars that raged for more than a decade.

If Nostradamus did have Napoleon in mind, he seems to have been taken by the emperor's short hair, referring to it more than once in his verses. In one verse, Nostradamus writes: "The man with short hair will assume authority/ In a maritime city held by the enemy./ He will expel the vile men who oppose him/ And for 14 years will rule with absolute power." Napoleon differed from the French kings preceding him by wearing his hair short, not long. In 1793, Napoleon entered the national spotlight by capturing the French maritime port of Toulon from occupying British. Napoleon went on to overthrow the corrupt Directory council which had been ruling during the French Revolution. Following a coup in 1799, Napoleon held absolute sway over France for the next 14 years.

Some commentators claim that Nostradamus came close to naming Napoleon. In verse 54 of Century 4, Nostradamus wrote: "Of the name which no Gallic King ever had/ Never was there so fearful a thunderbolt, Italy, Spain and the English trembling..." Some commentators note that, since the time of Nostradamus, the only crowned rulers of France to have a new name (not Henry, Louis or Charles, for example) were Napoleon I and his nephew Napoleon III. England was a principal foe of Napoleon, and Napoleon was involved in major, protracted fighting in Spain and Italy.

A intriguing but probably forced interpretation has even yielded Napoleon's name from verse 1 in Century 8. There, Nostradamus writes: "Pau, Nay, Oloron will be more of fire than blood..." Pau, Nay and Oloron are towns huddled closely together in southwest France. Yet the context of the verse indicates that Nostradamus is talking about a person, not geography. So, the 19th Century commentator H. Torn concluded that the three place names were a word jumble for Napoleon King (Napoleon roi), a quite controversial viewpoint.

Some say Nostradamus foresaw, in the following verse, Napoleon's exile to the Mediterranean island of Elba after his military defeat in 1814: "The captive prince, conquered, to Elba./ He will pass the Gulf of Genoa by sea to Marseilles/ He is completely conquered by a great effort of foreign forces/ Safe from gunshot, barrel of bee's liquor." For what it's worth, Napoleon did use bees as his emblem.

# The Masses Come to Power

As for the French Revolution, Nostradamus apparently did foresee this social upheaval two centuries in advance. In a prose preface to the *Centuries* written to his son Caesar, Nostradamus said he had been keeping his prophecies secret from the vulgar masses but had changed his mind. He was motivated to do so, he said, because of "the coming to power of the common people" (le commun avenement). As for specifics, some of his verses at least fit well with events before and during the revolution.

Many claim Nostradamus, in one verse, was thinking of the hedonistic and apathetic King Louis XV -- who reigned just before the revolution over an enormously suffering French peasantry and said the famous words, "After me, the flood." The seer wrote: "He who will succeed the great monarch on his death/ Will lead an illicit and wanton life:/ Through nonchalance he will give way to all/ So that in the end the Salic law will fail."

"The great monarch" would be an ideal designation for Louis XIV, the "Sun King" whose reign marked the peak of French kingship and who once said, "I am the nation." Louis XIV, of course, immediately preceded Louis XV. Some commentators have taken "Salic law will fail" as a symbol for the fall of the French monarchy, since the Salic law dealt with monarchial succession.

In Century 10, verse 43, Nostradamus talks about a king who is "too good" and doomed to die. Many commentators have applied this verse to the French King Louis XVI, fated to lose his head to the guillotine. Nostradamus writes: "Too much good times, too much of royal goodness,/ Ones made and unmade, quick, sudden, neglectful:/ Lightly will he believe falsely of his loyal wife,/ He put to death through his benevolence." The Nostradamus analyst Edgar Leoni notes that, as early as 1672, long before the affable, incompetent Louis XVI was even born, the commentator Garencieres wrote of this verse: "This is concerning another King, who through his too much goodness, simplicity and negligence, shall make and unmake those about him, and being fickle, shall believe false reports, made concerning his own wife; and at last by his too much goodness, shall be put to death." In fact, historians say Louis XVI was indeed a weak, irresolute king, lacking the ability to govern and neglecting state affairs, noted for, in the words of one commentator, "excessive kindness, which will leave him defenseless before his enemies." And Louis was quick to believe slanderous reports about the conduct of his wife, Marie Antoinette.

# Louis XVI's Flight and Capture

One of Nostradamus' most famous verses has been applied to the 1791 flight of Louis XVI from the French revolutionaries taking over his realm. Here is what Nostradamus wrote in the mid-1550s:

By night will come through the forest of "Reines,"
Two couples (some translate: "a married couple") round-about route Queen the white stone,
The monk king in gray in Varennes:
Elected Capet causes tempest, fire, blood, slice.

As for the first line, No "Forest of Reines" is known. However, various commentators believe that "forest" could be a typical Nostradamian pun, this time on the Latin word "fores" meaning door. "Reines," in turn, might refer to the French word "reine," which means "queen." Hence, these commentators have concluded that the words "forest of Reines" are a veiled way of saying "door of the queen." In fact, the royal couple did make a nighttime escape by coming through the queen's door.

As for line two, historians generally agree that the fleeing Louis and his queen took a poorly chosen and roundabout route. And the royal couple was in fact accompanied by Mme. de Tourzel and Count Fersen, making two couples. And if "Queen" is the proper translation of Nostradamus' word "Herne" (a legal anagram of reine. Nostradamus was an avid anagram buff), then Marie Antoinette could well be "the white stone" (Some commentators contend that the queen was dressed in white; others disagree). Various commentators have related "the white stone" to a famous diamond necklace which made the queen unpopular.

As for line three -- "the monk king in gray in Varennes" -- the king and queen were indeed captured in Varennes, an insignificant village, and Louis was wearing drab grey clothing and a broad-brimmed hat at the time of his arrest. Some commentators say the grey outfit made Louis look like a Carmelite monk. Others contend that the word "monk" actually alludes to the fact that Louis stood solitary, abandoned by his people in this grim stage of his life.

As to line 4, many see the phrase "elected Capet" as a well-fitting reference to Louis XVI. Capet is the name of an old French dynasty of kings and may simply have been used by Nostradamus to mean a French king. And Louis was the first French king to be elected by a constituent assembly rather than ruling by divine right alone, hence an "elected Capet." Historians have blamed Louis' weakness and indecision as a monarch for "causing" (i.e., strongly contributing to) the "tempest, fire and blood" of the French Revolution. Louis and his court lived high, borrowed heavily, and bankrupted the national treasury while the peasantry was mired in miserable poverty. When the short-of-cash king, to get financial help, was forced to convene the country's assembly, the Estates-General, this marked the rough beginning of the French Revolution. Line 4's last word "slice" is especially arresting, given Louis' ultimate fate on the guillotine.

## Nostradamus Sees England's Fate?

For some reason, Nostradamus, when he turned his attention to England, wrote substantially clearer, less murky prophecies. One of the most lucid and more credible may well be verse 37 of Century 9. Some analysts think Nostradamus was there foreseeing the beheading of the English King Charles 1 in the mid-1600s. Apparently with virtually no symbolism, Nostradamus plainly talks about an English king imprisoned near the Thames River in a fortress. At some point, the king, dressed in a simple shirt, faces death. Here is what Nostradamus said a century before Charles' execution:

The fortress near the Thames
Will fall when the King is locked up within:
Near the bridge in his shirt will be seen
One facing death, then barred in the fort

As commentators have noted, after King Charles' defeat in the English Civil War between royalists and Parliamentarians, the monarch was eventually imprisoned, in 1648, in Windsor Castle overlooking the Thames River. When Charles was taken out of the castle, he was put on trial. (Did the castle figuratively "fall" when it yielded up its royal occupant? The castle never literally fell during the civil war.) In January 1649, Charles wore a white shirt as he was executed. Some commentators think "near the bridge" might refer to London Bridge, although it was two miles downriver from where Charles died, as Leoni points out. The argument that Nostradamus had Charles I in mind is not hurt by this verse's obvious connection with verse 49 of Century 9, which baldly states: "The senate of London will put their king to death." Indeed, it was the English Parliament which condemned Charles.

As for England as a whole, Nostradamus was definitely optimistic. Although he lived more than a century before the birth of the British Empire, Nostradamus wrote: "The great empire shall be held by England,/ The all-powerful for more than 300 years;/ Great forces will pass by land and sea,/ The Portuguese will not be pleased." As it turned out, the British Empire was considered by many historians to have been born with the Navigation Act of 1651. Indeed, the British Empire lasted just over 300 years, breaking up in the 20 years following World War II. Yet, at the time Nostradamus wrote, the only great European colonial powers were Portugal and Spain. Certainly, the Portuguese "were not pleased" by the growing British Empire, which seriously restricted Portuguese world trade, especially in India.

The above prophecies show, as no words can, how tantalizing and suggestive yet discouragingly inconclusive Nostradamus can be. Nothing could better illustrate the controversy caused by this vagueness than a verse which made Nostradamus an overnight sensation in France.

# Death of Henry II

In 1559, Nostradamus' growing reputation among French nobles as a gifted seer suddenly soared when King Henry II was mortally wounded during a friendly joust with the captain of his Scottish guards. The royal court immediately thought of one of Nostradamus' verses:

> The young lion will overcome the old
> On the field of war in single combat
> He will put out his eyes in a cage of gold
> Two wounds one, then he dies a cruel death

The jousting tragedy occurred when the captain's lance accidentally struck the king, splintering. Henry was wounded in the neck and a fragment of the lance also penetrated his supposedly gilded helmet visor ("the cage of gold"), piercing him behind the right eye. After days of agony, the 40-year-old Henry died. Montmorency shouted: "Cursed be the divine who predicted it so evilly and so well," although he may not have had in mind Nostradamus but an Italian astrologer, Luc Gauric. Three years earlier, Gauric had written the king to warn him "to avoid all single combat in an enclosed place, especially near his forty-first year, for in that period of his life, he was menaced by a wound in the head which might rapidly result in blindness or even in death." Gauric's letter has been well documented by historians. In fact, Henry commented on the prophecy at the time, saying that he was basically indifferent about his manner of death but would actually prefer a death in combat as long as he died honorably at the hands of a brave man.

Despite the Gauric prophecy, it was Nostradamus' published verse supposedly referring to King Henry that was soon the talk of France. French high society was struck by the correspondences it saw in Nostradamus' verse and what actually happened during and after the joust. The 34-year-old captain of the guard and the 40-year-old king were considered the "young lion" and the "old lion." Commentators have disputed whether they actually both used the lion as their emblems. Nostradamus supporters have maintained that the king suffered a wound in the area of the eye, after a "cage of gold" (gilded helmet) was pierced. The tournament joust amounted

113

to "single combat" on a figurative "field of war," resulting in a "cruel" death for Henry, who died in agony 10 days later. And the "old lion" was indeed wounded twice during the joust, in the neck and face.

Nostradamus critics, however, have adroitly counter-attacked. They say the age difference between the guard and the king was actually quite slight for "old" and "young" lions, only six years. They also point out that Nostradamus' original word "classes," translated as "wounds" in line four, is consistently used elsewhere by Nostradamus to mean a fleet of ships. They also contend that the king's visor was not golden or gilded and the "eye wound" was actually above the eye. Furthermore, other Nostradamus verses were seemingly predicting a rosy future for Henry as a "new Charlemagne."

Whatever the case may be, Queen Catherine de Medicis was so impressed by the verse that she summoned Nostradamus to the royal court after the tragedy and Nostradamus' international reputation was assured. Nostradamus' son Caesar said that Parisians were so incensed at what they felt was Nostradamus' prediction of the royal death that they burned the seer in effigy.

## The Source of Nostradamus' Power

If Nostradamus, unlike everyday prophets, really could see centuries, not just hours or days, into the future, where was this alleged gift supposed to have come from? Nostradamus himself credited divine inspiration, astrology and inherited powers. The keen-witted Nostradamus had consulted many alchemists, scholars and seers during his six years of wanderings over France and Italy, apparently accumulating esoteric lore with his outstanding memory. In fact, while composing the *Centuries*, the seer was said to stare for hours each night into a water-filled bowl to see the future, probably a form of scrying. Nevertheless, some Nostradamus observers contend that all his hocus pocus was mere window dressing for simple clairvoyant ability, present on a smaller scale in ordinary people.

Whatever his powers, if any, no one can deny that Nostradamus has been proven wrong. For example, he forecast that the year 1732 would climax a chain of natural disasters which would almost exterminate humankind. Nothing of the sort happened. He also was wrong in his prediction that violent religious persecution would be under way in 1792. Nostradamus was both wrong and right about his own death. He had a standing prediction that he would die in November 1567, but by July 1, 1566, sick with gout and dropsy, the 62-year-old seer summoned a priest to hear his confession. That night, a visitor took his leave from Nostradamus with a polite traditional farewell, saying, "Until tomorrow." Nostradamus replied: "You will not find me alive at sunrise." The seer was found dead in the following predawn hours.

And yet despite Nostradamus' obvious errors, despite his murky prophetic style, the barrage of well-aimed criticism from Nostradamus-debunkers, the bulk of the Nostradamus evidence has convinced some reasonably objective observers that Nostradamus did have a gift of some sort. Possibly an extraordinary one. We will never know for sure. Nostradamus saw to that with his anagrams, puns, and the like.

Upper left: The French physician Michel de Nostredame, better known as Nostradamus, allegedly displayed the greatest prophetic powers the modern world has seen. Lower right: Catherine de Medicis, the wily Queen of France, was so impressed with Nostradamus that she summoned him to the royal court.

**Nostradamus apparently did foresee the French Revolution two centuries in advance, referring to the social upheaval as "the coming to power of the common people." As for specifics, some of his verses at least fit well with events before and during the revolution. Illustrated above is the storming by a revolutionary mob of the Bastille, a hated Parisian prison fortress and symbol of royal political terror.**

Several of Nostradamus' verses sound intriguingly like descriptions of Napoleon. Here, the French dictator receives the queen of Prussia.

# Colorful Prophets

The prophets of history have been a diversity of intriguing, colorful or just plain strange individuals: a village idiot, sleeping prophet, and a Nazi propagandist, to cite a few. The membership in this gallery of seers includes:

* The world-famous Victorian palmist and adventurer Louis Hamon. He predicted King Edward VIII's abdication to marry a divorcee, impressed the arch-skeptic Mark Twain, and once allegedly got into a hypnosis contest with the Russian Mad Monk Rasputin.

* The prophesying village idiot of the 1400s, Robert Nixon. A prophetic idiot-savant, he spent most of his time as a retarded plowboy. But he did have moments of mental lucidity when he prophesied so accurately that he came to the king's attention, unfortunately for Nixon.

* The so-called "Sleeping Prophet," mild-mannered photographer Edgar Cayce, who went into trances and made predictions, with mixed results. While entranced, Cayce also successfully diagnosed and treated tens of thousands of medical ailments despite the limitations of a sixth-grade education. Among Cayce's best known predictions is his forecast for massive and devastating geological upheavals from 1958 to 1998.

* Karl Ernst Krafft and Louis de Wohl, two astrologers who waged their own variety of "Star Wars" during World War II. They produced competing propagandistic "prophecies" about the fates of the Allies and the Axis.

* England's leading astrologer of the 1600s, William Lilly. Lilly's repeated prediction of the great London plague and fire of 1665 and 1666 caused authorities to suspect he may have had a role in setting the fire, but he was exonerated.
* Evangeline Adams, America's "female Nostradamus." Put on trial in New York City for fortune-telling, she was acquitted after casting a "blind" horoscope for the judge's son.

## Cheiro: Palmist of kings

In his youth, Louis Hamon began an adventurous life by leaving his native Ireland and studying palmistry under an Indian guru for three years. His palmistry text supposedly was written on human skin. Eventually arriving in London, Hamon set up a sumptious salon in a fashionable London district to tell fortunes by palmistry, numerology and astrology. Falsely passing himself off as a count with a distinguished lineage going back to the Norman conquest, Hamon soon attracted rich and famous customers from all over the world, eventually including the king of England and the American President Grover Cleveland. Hamon's reputation was greatly boosted when he publicly warned the shah of Persia that his life was in danger. The shah, at the time, was about to attend the Paris Exposition of 1900. The shah's prime minister beefed up security, and soon after, an anarchist appeared trying to shoot the shah but was overpowered. The grateful monarch decorated Hamon.

The brilliant, charming and dashing Hamon was a lady killer. One client claims that during World War 1, he worked secretly for British intelligence, taking the notorious German spy and nude dancer Mata Hari as a lover.

In his *Note Book*, the famous skeptic of the supernatural, Samuel Clemens, known better by his pen name Mark Twain, recorded how he came to Hamon. At the time, Clemens wrote, he was in dire financial straits, heavily in debt, because of poor investments. Clemens wrote that Hamon predicted he would become rich from an unexpected source in his 68th year. In fact, Clemens said, he was nine days shy of turning 68 when he signed a lucrative contract with a publisher, guaranteeing himself a princely annual income. After one particular visit to Hamon, Clemens wrote in the palmist's visitor's book: "Cheiro (the palmist's professional name: Greek for "hand") has exposed my character to me with humiliating accuracy. I ought not to confess this accuracy, still I am moved to do it."

One of Hamon's most celebrated predictions was published in 1925. He wrote of the then prince of Wales, Edward: "It is within the range of possibility, owing to the peculiar planetary influences to which he is subject, that he will fall victim of a devastating love affair. If he does, I predict that the prince will give up everything, rather than lose the object of his affection." Eleven years later, in 1936, Edward was crowned king of England. But he later abdicated his throne rather than let British officials stop him from marrying the twice-divorced commoner, Wallis Warfield Simpson.

In 1892, Hamon was challenged at a London party to read a palm "blind," with the owner concealed behind a curtain. It turned out to be the internationally celebrated writer and wit Oscar Wilde. Hamon warned Wilde, then 38, that he faced ruin in his 41st or 42nd year. Within three years, Wilde was accused by the Marquess of Queensberry of having an affair with her son. Wilde's homosexuality trial was a major scandal in Victorian England and he was imprisoned.

Hamon was a public relations genius and this shows in the colorful stories recounted in his memoirs, for some of which we unfortunately have only his word. For example, Hamon contended that he foresaw the doom of Rasputin, the "Mad Monk" who had the czar and his family under his influence. Hamon claimed he made a secret trip to Russia in 1904, where he dined with Czar Nicholas II. During the meal, Hamon supposedly reiterated his prediction of a coming Russian Revolution that would destroy the czar's Romanov dynasty.

Hamon, incidentally, maintained that he did not directly get information about his clients from their palm lines or horoscopes. Rather, he asserted that the lines and the star charts stimulated his "occult consciousness" (clairvoyance?) to provide answers about the future.

Perhaps appropriately, the flamboyant Hamon spent his last years in Hollywood, California, in the 1930s, at a time when his powers supposedly were failing him.

# The Cheshire Idiot and the King

Robert Nixon, called the "Cheshire Idiot," was a retarded rural plowboy who became a voice of prophecy for the English King Henry VII. Henry supposedly had a scribe follow Nixon around the palace recording his words. Nixon's saga began when fellow laborers are said to have heard him uttering occasional monologues with himself in poetic meter, despite the fact that at other times, the slobbering Nixon could barely talk. One day, a plowing Nixon was suddenly heard to exclaim: "Now, Dick! Now, Harry! Oh, ill done, Dick! Oh, well done, Harry. Harry has gained the day!"

The next day, Nixon's village of Over supposedly learned from hard-riding messengers that, at the time of Nixon's exclamation, the wicked hunchback King Richard III had been killed in battle, and Henry, the earl of Richmond, had been proclaimed ruler of England. Nixon's spreading fame soon caused the new king to send for him. Nixon was clairvoyantly aware beforehand that a king's summons was on the way. He became extremely upset, running around, announcing that the king was sending for him and he would eventually be "clammed" -- a slang term for "starved to death."

When Nixon arrived at court, Henry is said to have tested his powers by faking distress at having lost a valuable diamond. Actually, the king had merely concealed the jewel himself. Asked about the whereabouts of the "lost" ring, Nixon startled his liege by quoting a proverb: "Those who hide can find."

Nixon allegedly foretold events ranging from the British Civil War of the 1600s to the great London fire of 1666. But in the end, his own fatal prophecy about himself supposedly came true. Nixon kept asking the king to let him go or he would starve. Henry reacted by ordering that Nixon be given all the food he wanted. According to one account, the ever-hungry Nixon was an irritation to the palace servants, despite his status as a royal favorite. One day, while the king was away hunting, the royal cooks locked up the bothersome prophet inside a closet and soon forgot he was there. Back from his hunt, the king asked for the royal pronosticator. He was found still in the closet, dead from lack of food and water.

# The "Star Wars" of World War II

An astrological "Star Wars" developing between Britain and Germany during World War II traced its beginning to a Swiss astrologer's warning about Adolph Hitler's safety. On Nov. 2, 1939, the astrologer, Karl Ernst Krafft, sent his warning to German intelligence. Krafft said he had cast a horoscope for Adolph Hitler which indicated that the fuehrer faced great danger from Nov. 7 to Nov. 10. Krafft wrote that there was the "possibility of an attempt of assassination by the use of explosive material." Krafft's prediction was ignored by a minor bureaucrat and not passed up the chain of command. As it turned out, though, on Nov. 8, shortly after Hitler had prematurely left a Nazi meeting at Munich, a hidden bomb exploded and wrecked the speaker's platform, killing seven. Krafft telegramed Hitler's second-in-command, Rudolph Hess, to call the attention of top Nazis to his successful prophecy, which was still on file, gathering dust at the intelligence agency. Hitler was apparently alarmed by Krafft's accuracy. Indeed, Gestapo agents assumed Krafft had been part of the plot. But the astrologer finally convinced his dogged interrogators that he was innocent by demonstrating how he had calculated Hitler's horoscope and interpreted it. Instead of executing him, the Nazis hired Krafft to use astrology in waging psychological warfare against the British.

Krafft soon set to work reinterpreting the hard-to-understand prophetic verses of the 16th Century seer Nostradamus. Krafft's analysis twisted Nostradamus into forecasting a Nazi victory. Krafft also repeatedly cast horoscopes for such major Third Reich enemies as the British leader Winston Churchill and the American President Franklin Roosevelt, naturally predicting bleak futures for them. Away from his government job, though, Krafft's private predictions to sympathetic Nazis in the spring of 1940 turned out to be far closer to the truth. Krafft privately predicted that Germany would be winning until the winter of 1942-43 but after that, the Reich would face a very unfavorable future. Krafft advised these Nazis that Germany should conclude a peace with the Allies before 1942, while the Reich was still victorious. History bore out Krafft's words: With successive blitzkriegs, Germany overran Western Europe in 1940. In 1941 and 1942, the Germans advanced relentlessly eastward through the Soviet Union. But then, in January 1943, the tide turned. A half-frozen army of 300,000 Germans was encircled at Stalingrad, and only 91,000 emaciated soldiers survived to surrender to the Russians.

Nevertheless, it was not Krafft's private views but events beyond his control that brought him down. In 1941, Hess, the deputy fuehrer of the Nazi Party, acted on his own in flying to Scotland to attempt to negotiate an end to the war. The British simply jailed him after he landed. Meanwhile, in Germany, the embarrassed Nazi leadership realized that Hess had been influenced to make his trip by astrological forecasts. Thus, a massive crackdown began on astrology in the Third Reich. Krafft, among the astrologers arrested, was thrown into solitary confinement for a year. After that, Krafft was ordered to produce a horoscope interpretation unfavorable to President Franklin Roosevelt. Thinking he would be freed for cooperating, Krafft abused astrological rules to produce a contrived horoscope "proving" that Roosevelt was a dupe of Wall Street and "international Jewry." Krafft soon began to realize that he would not be released, stopped cooperating and was finally put in a concentration camp. He died in 1945 of typhus while being transferred by train to the horrible Nazi death camp at Buchenwald.

During the course of Nazi astrological warfare, the Allies were not idle. The British military did not believe in astrology but they did think that Hitler was being counseled by an astrologer and might be taking some of the advice. So the British hired a part-Jewish, refugee Hungarian astrologer, Louis de Wohl, to try to predict what kind of advice Hitler was supposedly getting. Actually, though, Hitler had little interest in astrology until the Third Reich was collapsing in 1945.

At any rate, de Wohl's new Psychological Research Bureau produced horoscopes to show how the war would proceed and what Hitler might do. The British also subsidized the publication of De Wohl's pro-Allied horoscopes worldwide to counter pro-Nazi horoscopes being published internationally.

In April 1945, as the Third Reich was collapsing, Hitler's propaganda chief Joseph Goebbels and the dictator himself discussed horoscopes for Hitler and Germany. Prepared by Nazi researchers, these horoscopes had earlier successfully predicted the beginning of World War II in 1939, German conquests up to 1941 and defeats thereafter. However, the horoscopes also predicted an overpowering victory by the Germans in April 1945, with peace to come in August, a buoyant Goebbels told his fuehrer. However, within a fortnight of this discussion, Goebbels had an SS orderly shoot him and his wife, while Hitler turned a gun on himself. The Reich went on to be crushed by the Allies in May.

## Cayce: The Sleeping Prophet

Unlike many other prophets who were a flash in the pan, mostly forgotten beyond their day, the Kentucky-born photographer turned psychic, Edgar Cayce, is still a household word almost a half century after his death in 1945. Many consider him America's greatest 20th Century psychic. In his youth, the gentle and meek photographer discovered that, while entranced, he could psychically diagnose and prescribe treatment for ailing patients. Although a sixth grade dropout with zero medical knowledge, Cayce went on to diagnose the ailments of tens of thousands of often difficult patients with startling accuracy. His prescriptions, frequently offbeat, obsolete or unheard of, lead to what many of his patients considered cures. Among his early successes were his son, cured of serious eye damage that doctors had considered hopeless, and his wife, cured of a life-threatening case of tuberculosis. Coming out of his trances, Cayce could not remember what had transpired. Many times, he could not even understand the things he had been discussing, which included technical medical jargon.

During the course of his healing "readings," as he called them, Cayce began to report, in an incidental way, on the futures of the sitters in question as well as on future events in general. Six months before the October 1929 stock market crash, Cayce told friends to sell all their stock because a coming crash would lead to a depression. Cayce also predicted in 1939 that two American presidents would die in office during times of racial strife. Kennedy's death in the 1960s civil rights era of racial strife and Franklin Roosevelt's death in 1945 are cited by Cayce supporters as fulfillment of that prophecy. Some claim that the Pacific war between the oriental Japanese and the occidental Americans amounted to "racial strife" in Roosevelt's time. Meanwhile, as Stalin's terror gripped the

Soviet Union, Cayce asserted that that atheistic, totalitarian country would one day become democratized and respiritualized -- "the greater hope of the world" and a friend of the United States. This does sound strangely like what has started happening in the late 1980s.

Cayce's most sensational predictions call for a cycle of violent geologic changes that are to rock the earth during the years from 1958 to 1998, mostly in the latter part of the 40-year era. Among the dire prophecies:

* California will break off from the North American continent and slide into the sea.
* Japan will also sink.
* New York will be destroyed.
* The fabled Lost Continent of Atlantis will rise.

Evidence of Atlantis was supposed to have come in the late 1960s, according to Cayce. Cayce predicted that land would at that time surface out of water off the Florida coast near Bimini to provide the evidence, but that did not happen. As for the predicted cataclysmic 40-year "earth changes," Cayce supporters claim that earthquake activity has already been unusual around the world. However, there certainly seems to date to be no real confirmation of any globally devastating "earth changes," as Cayce called them.

All in all, Cayce's impressive healing career seems to have generated more acceptance than his role as a prophet. Critics of Cayce attack his prophetic "hits" -- such as his prediction in the 1930s of the coming of World War II -- as lucky or logical guesses. Cayce's prediction of a stock market crash six months before it occurred, when a bull market had been under way for years, was not particularly spectacular, they claim. And Cayce has been wrong, they note. For example, in 1943, he foresaw a Christianized, democratic China by the late 1960s. As for predicted "earth changes," time has not yet run out on Cayce's four -decade timetable.

As a Christian fundamentalist and daily Bible reader, Cayce was disturbed when his entranced self began giving reincarnation-style past life readings for sitters, although he finally accepted the idea of multiple lives. Whatever the validity of reincarnation, these past life readings eventually turned Cayce's attention to Atlantis. His set of readings on the fabled lost continent are perhaps the most controversial he produced. Cayce saw Atlantis as a huge continent in the Atlantic, peopled by a strong-willed, technologically advanced race that used death rays, nuclear power, and also relied for energy on a "Terrible Crystal." As Cayce told it, materialists controlling Atlantis accidentally misused the Terrible Crystal to destructively focus solar energy, setting off volcanic eruptions that completely sank Atlantis into the Caribbean Sea in 10,000 B.C. Cayce was apparently sincere about all this, but no evidence has ever turned up for any of Cayce's Atlantis claims.

Cayce would slip into a trance by lying on a couch, folding his palms over his torso and breathing heavily. When his eyelids began fluttering, an assistant would make an hypnotic-like suggestion to begin the "reading" session. Cayce would then delve into his subconscious to tap what was called "universal knowledge." In all, Cayce gave at least 30,000 readings in his lifetime, more than 14,000 of them well documented, generally refusing to profit from his psychic gift for fear of losing it. In fact, the crush of his schedule has been blamed for his death. By 1944, Cayce was physically deteriorating at a time when 1,500 requests a day for help were pouring in, some of them desperate pleas. The emaciated Cayce refused to slow his pace. On New Year's Day 1945, the 67-year-old Cayce cheerfully remarked to visitors: "It is all arranged. I am to be healed on Friday, the fifth of January." Cayce's meaning became clear to his friends when, on Jan. 5, they attended the sleeping prophet's funeral. He had died two days earlier.

## Lilly Asked About London Fire

Back in the 1600s, the seer William Lilly demonstrated that being a prophet of doom can be especially hazardous when the sufferers wonder whether you are just a prophet or actually an instigator of the calamity. Much of the fame of Lilly, considered by some the leading astrologer of the 1600s, was built on the fact that he seemed to explicitly predict a great plague and fire that were a double whammy for London in 1665 and 1666. In fact, his published predictions of plague and fire for the city were so accurate that he was called before a suspicious Parliament and interrogated to determine if he actually was part of a conspiracy to set the fire.

Events began in 1648 when Lilly published the almanac **Astrological Predictions**. In the almanac, Lilly wrote that celestial signs indicated that a "strange catastrophe of human affairs" was in store for London either around the year 1656 or within 10 years of that date. Lilly added that this unprecedented "revolution of fate" would be "ominous to London, unto her merchants at sea, to her traffique at land, to her poor, to her rich, to all sorts of people inhabiting in her... by reason of sundry fires and a consuming plague."

Then, in 1651, Lilly underscored all this by publishing another work which contained certain woodcut illustrations. These illustrations, Lilly contended, portrayed the ills awaiting London. One set of woodcuts showed corpses wrapped in sheets as well as graves being dug. All of this symbolized "a great sickness and mortality," in Lilly's words. Another illustration showed citizen firefighters battling a blazing fire as a pair of twins descended toward the inferno. The twins symbolized the constellation Gemini, the zodiacal sign of London.

Beginning in the summer of 1665, bubonic plague did rage through filthy London for six months, killing almost 70,000 people. A little more than a year later, at 3 a.m. on Sept. 2, 1666, while the capital was still reeling from the 1665 disaster, a fire started in a London baker's shop. Stiff winds spread the blaze rapidly through three hot and dry summer days until two thirds of mostly wooden London was destroyed, leaving 200,000 homeless but killing only six. Meanwhile, a committee of Parliament's House of Commons remembered "the precision with which (Lilly) was thought to have foretold the event," as one commentator put it, and suspected that the astrologer may well have been part of a plot to deliberately set the fire. Under questioning, Lilly satisfied the parliamentarians that his foreknowledge of the twin disasters was purely astrological, and he was "dismissed with great civility."

By now, Lilly was the most-recognized Englishman next to the king himself. A horoscope analyst for nobleman and commoner alike, he made as many as 2,000 consultations a year. Once, he scanned the stars for King Charles I, defeated in the English Civil War, to recommend the best place to hide should he escape prison. Among other things, Lilly was also credited with predicting that the English masses would one day undo Parliament. He wrote in 1651 that "Parliament stood upon a tottering foundation, and that the commonalty and soldiery would join together against them." This was considered fulfilled when the English dictator Oliver Cromwell, who led the middle and lower classes to victory over the nobility in the Civil War, arbitrarily purged Parliament of members opposing him.

## Mother Shipton: the Forgers

Our next prophet, Mother Shipton, may be more interesting as an example of the pitfalls of chronicling prophecy than for her story itself. To begin with, historians cannot even agree whether this supposed English prophetess of the 1500s really existed or was pure fable. Her reputation is based entirely on folk tales, legends, and deliberately forged "prophecies." The most galling of these forgeries began circulating in an 1862 pamphlet published by the British book-seller Charles Hindley. Hindley claimed he was reprinting the prophecy from an earlier 1684 pamphlet. The prophecy went like this:

"Carriages without horses shall go
And accidents fill the world with woe.
Around the earth thoughts shall fly
In the twinkling of an eye...
Through hills man shall ride
And no horse be at his side...
Iron in the water shall float
As easily as a wooden boat...
The world to an end shall come
In eighteen hundred and eighty-one.

This certainly was an astounding 16th Century prophecy in the eyes of 19th Century Victorians acquainted with the recent invention of the telegraph, the train and iron ships and anticipating new technological wonders like "horseless carriages." Alas, in 1873, Hindley confessed that he forged it. Nevertheless, the prophecy continued to be publicized as genuine and repeatedly discussed well into the 20th Century by many authors unaware of Hindley's shenanigans. This, despite the obviously modern poetical style, seemingly at odds with language to be expected from a 1684 pamphlet. The problem of undocumented "retroactive prophecies" (made after the fact but publicized as genuine) and their credulous acceptance is still one of the skeptic's most frequent arguments against genuine precognition.

According to legend, as a girl, Mother Shipton was tormented by jeering children because of her freakish looks, including bulging eyes. Curiously, early pamphlet illustrations of Mother Shipton show her with the hooked nose, humped back and chin characteristic of Mr. Punch in the centuries-old Punch and Judy show of wandering puppeteers. Some commentators, for various reasons, believe Mother Shipton may have been a model for Punch.

The Mother Shipton prophecy which supposedly won her a national reputation concerned Cardinal Thomas Wolsey, the powerful right-hand man of England's bloody King Henry VIII. In 1529, she predicted that Wolsey, then on his way to settle in York, would see the city but never actually arrive there. Supposedly, Wolsey got close enough to view York from a distance, but the cardinal's trip was then cut short by orders from the king to face treason charges in London. Wolsey's real crime was failing to arrange a quick divorce for King Henry from the first of his six wives. Beginning about 80 years after Mother Shipton's death, different writers expanded the prophetess' credits to include suspect prophecies of everything from the Great Fire of London in 1666 to the defeat of the Spanish Armada in 1588.

## America's "Female Nostradamus"

Better documented are the exploits of the early 20th Century astrologer Evangeline Adams, nicknamed "America's female Nostradamus." In 1899, Adams created a national sensation shortly after moving to New York and checking into a room at the stately Windsor Hotel on Fifth Avenue. She cast a horoscope for the hotel owner and predicted a disaster "terrifying in its unfriendliness" that would occur almost immediately. The owner knew of no imminent dangers, assumed Mrs. Adams was a quack, and did nothing. But that day, the hotel burned to the ground, killing the hotelier's wife and taking with it many of Adams' belongings. The anguished proprietor told what had happened to the press and instantly, head-lines carried the story of Adams' prediction from coast to coast. In 1914, Adams' career got another boost, in an unusual way. That year, the astrologer was arrested in New York for fortune-telling, but she spurned the idea of paying a fine and insisted on a trial. In the courtroom, she defended herself by explaining how she inter-preted horoscopes, and she offered to cast a horoscope from the birth date of someone she had never met and to analyze it. The horoscope turned out to be that of the judge's son. Judge John H. Freschi is often quoted as having approvingly declared: "The defen-dant has raised astrology to the dignity of an exact science." Actually, what the judge meant, legally speaking, was that Adams **contended** at her trial that astrology had the dignity of an exact science." At any rate, Adams was acquitted. She came to be regarded as America's most popular astrologer, star-gazing for such powerful or famous figures as the industrialist J.P. Morgan, the singer Caruso and England's King Edward VII. By the early 1930s, the wealthy Adams was getting 4,000 requests a day to cast horoscopes. Adams con-tinued as a national celebrity through the 1930s and early 1940s, writ-ing books and conducting radio programs.

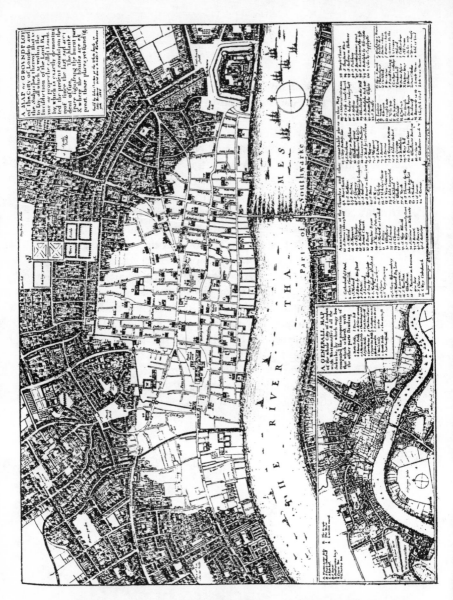

Astrologer William Lilly was called before a suspicious Parliament to explain his seeming foreknowledge of the great plague and fire that ravaged London in 1665 and 1666. Above, a contemporary map shows the extent of the fire damage.

The prophesying village idiot of the 1400s, Robert Nixon, began a process that led to his doom when he announced the victory of Henry II (above left) over the evil King Richard III (above right). Below: Cardinal Thomas Wolsey, mentioned in the Mother Shipton legends.

Not just the land, sea and air, but even the stars themselves were battlegrounds for the Axis and Allies during World War II as each side tried to use astrology as a weapon. Shown on this page is a medieval woodcut depicting the constellations of the northern sky. At each corner is a famous astronomer, including Ptolemy at upper right.

# Everyone a Prophet

Most people assume that only a mystic elite can see the future. But the evidence is that everyone has this gift to some degree. Indeed, on one occasion, more than half of those responding to a *London Times* poll told the upscale newspaper that they believed they had had at least one personal precognitive experience.

With most people, though, prophetic powers are latent and undeveloped. When ordinary people foresee the future, they usually do so unconsciously, as shown by a mid-1950s study by researcher W. E. Cox. Cox surveyed 28 American railroad accidents in which at least 10 persons were hurt. He found that the trains consistently carried significantly fewer passengers on the days of the wrecks, a phenomenon he labeled "accident avoidance." Moreover, the damaged and derailed coaches themselves carried fewer passengers than would have been expected. Cox theorized that some passengers might have subconsciously foreseen the wrecks and changed their travel plans, without ever realizing the real reason why.

In fact, ESP in general seems to be used by ordinary people unconsciously. There is evidence that a continual telepathic chatter is going on between the minds of ordinary, "non-psychic" people, but all of this on an unconscious level. This exchanged knowledge seldom rises into conscious awareness. However, the telepathic linkup apparently accounts for many coincidences, such as "lucky breaks" or fortunate chance meetings. In his book *The Roots of Consciousness*, Jeffrey Mishlove cites the story of a retired army colonel who found himself unthinkingly departing the New York subway at an incorrect exit. He immediately chanced to run into the very people he wanted to visit. Mishlove goes on to report research by Rex Stanford into this interesting use of unconscious ESP. In one experiment, Stanford administered an essay test to psychology students. He gave each one

135

a sealed, opaque envelope which contained the answers to half of the test's questions. But the students were misled into believing that the envelopes contained carbon paper. After the scoring, the students were found to have done better on the questions which had corresponding answers inside the sealed envelopes, as if the students had unconsciously used clairvoyance to see the answers. What's more, researcher Martin Johnson at Sweden's Lund University conducted a similar experiment in which the sealed answers were wrong. His students did poorer on the corresponding questions. "If we carry this line of thought a little further," Mishlove writes, "it becomes reasonable to assume that all of the important coincidences in our lives were actually psi-mediated."

Was the war-era British prime minister, Winston Churchill, acting on an unconscious prophetic impulse during a tour of London one night? On the trip, some inner urge of Churchill's impelled him to sit on the opposite side of a car from his customary place. Then, on the Kingston Bypass, a bomb exploded on Churchill's side of the car, raising it up momentarily onto two wheels, but the vehicle righted itself. Churchill later kidded that his "beef" had kept the car from tipping over. An overturning of the car would certainly have killed this charismatic leader desperately needed by the British in their fight against Hitler.

And speaking of Hitler, here was another candidate for the mantle of unconscious seer. During World War I, after dreaming of being buried, Corporal Adolph Hitler inexplicably scurried away from a battlefield trench seconds before a shell struck, killing and burying all his fellow soldiers. As reported in the last chapter, the fascist fanatic later escaped a bomb in 1939 by prematurely leaving a Munich Nazi meeting. Later in the war, a surprising series of probably synchronistic "coincidences" enabled this despot with nine lives to escape one assassination attempt after another.

Another thing keeping prophecy on mostly an unconscious level with ordinary people is the widespread lack of belief in it or even fear of it. Indeed, the repressing of precognitive and other psi ability seems to explain a curious phenomenon of ESP experiments. Namely, in the parapsychological laboratory, skeptics are known to often consistently score **below** chance in such experiments.

# Recording a Town's Dreams

Dreams are a common way in which precognitive knowledge does reach the conscious minds of ordinary people. In fact, as reported in the October 1989 *Body Mind & Spirit* magazine, one woman, Susan Watkins, decided to systematically record the dreams of her fellow residents in the small town of Dundee, New York. Watkins was looking for signs of precognition in the dreams. "As Watkins becomes the unofficial dream shaman of her town, she finds astonishing correlations -- though not in the way she expected," reports Carol Kramer, who reviewed Watkins' book, *Dreaming Myself, Dreaming a Town*. "Precognitive indicators that appear in the dreams of the townspeople of deaths, accidents, etc. are shrouded in symbolism -- always correct but rarely useful to the rational mind ahead of time," Kramer wrote. Watkins discovered that separate individuals, unacquainted with one another, would contribute pieces of information that fit together to describe a coming event, an event always recognizable only with hindsight.

Not only does everyone appear to be capable of prophecy at least unconsciously, but many believe that conscious prophesying is a learned skill anyone can pick up. Some budding prophets keep dream diaries. Others use auto-suggestion or self-hypnosis to instruct themselves to become aware of fleeting precognitive feelings. The leading prophet Alan Vaughan observes in his 1982 book *The Edge of Tomorrow* that student seers, when they begin their work, are more successful predicting colors, emotions, and images -- all processed by the dreamy intuitive right brain -- than names, dates and numbers, processed by the rational left brain.

But prophecy and psychic powers are definitely not for everybody. Sociologist Laile Bartlett quotes one clinical psychologist as contending that there were 2,000 cases of persons requiring psychotherapy because they had prematurely tried to force psychic powers in themselves.

# Prophecy and Self-Growth

Still, prophecy has often helped its practitioners -- among other things, in the area of self-growth. Consider a strange case in 1909 which involved the two giants of 20th Century psychiatry, Sigmund Freud and Carl Jung. The two were having a disagreement. The skeptical Freud was warning the mystic-oriented Jung about becoming overwhelmed by the "black mud of occultism." Jung suddenly felt a red-hot sensation in his abdomen. At that moment, a loud crack suddenly came from the area of a bookcase. Jung claimed that his inner abdominal feeling and the cracking sound were connected. Freud replied that Jung's idea was nonsense. As Jung was insisting he was right, he suddenly knew, beforehand, that another explosion was coming, and he told Freud so. A second explosion did follow immediately. Freud was emotionally shaken by the experience, which no doubt softened his skepticism about Jung's innovative ideas and led to personal intellectual growth.

On another occasion, thanks to prophecy, Jung achieved a breakthrough in his psychiatric treatment of an extremely skeptical, rationalistic patient. The woman patient had dreamed of a golden scarab beetle, rare in the area where she and Jung lived. The next day, as the two discussed this beetle, Jung heard a rapping against his window. Jung opened it and a beetle nearly identical to the dream scarab flew inside the office. Jung grabbed the beetle and offered it to his patient as proof that cold, logical science cannot explain everything in the world. This led to a breakthrough in her attitude. Again, precognition had worked to further self-development.

Father Time sets the clock to start the new year 1889, which emerges young and fresh into the present out of the mists of the future. Shadowy, still-to-come years wait behind 1889 for their turn to arrive in the present. Meanwhile, the hooded and shrouded old year 1888, stooped with age, shuffles out of the present into the mists of the past, joining even older years ahead of it.

Research suggests that prophetic powers are used by the psychic and "non-psychic" alike. A case in point was the German literary giant Wolfgang Goethe, who claimed he saw a vision of his future self, as he would be eight years later.

Dreams are a common way for a person's subconscious knowledge of the future to reach the conscious mind. Above, the ancient Hebrew youth Joseph tells his older brothers he has dreamed that he will one day be a great person. The angry brothers reacted by selling Joseph into slavery, but he went on to become the Egyptian pharaoh's chief administrator, according to Bible legend.

# Finding Your Fate

The idea that we are all prophets has not been radical enough for some observers. They go further and claim that each of us has a subconscious "plan" for the future events of our lives. Some persons, say students of prophecy, eventually discover their hidden blueprint, their "purpose in life," and build their lives accordingly, finding happiness. They may be guided to discover that subconscious blueprint by considering their inborn talents, their youthful ambitions, hunches, guiding dreams, even synchronistic "coincidences" that steer them in certain directions, the thinking goes. Others never find the subconscious master plan, or resist it, and lead lives of frustration. Perhaps, the real plan for a life may have shown itself as a teen-age ambition that was later rejected as "impractical." Or the plan required too much work and remained forever an unfulfilled idle "wish."

Nevertheless, the great philosopher Ralph Waldo Emerson noted that any longheld and cherished ambition amounts to an intuitive, "inner proof" that the person harboring such a goal is capable of achieving it. Or as the author James Allen put it so eloquently at the turn of the century: "The Vision that you glorify in your mind, the Ideal that you enthrone in your heart, this you will build your life by. This you will become."

How can you know that you have found your path? "You know... from the feedback you get... Life becomes more exciting and satisfying, opportunities come, and there is more of an ease to things," wrote psychic Alan Vaughan.

## A Scientist Escapes a Labor Camp

Once you have firmly and decisively found your hidden future, it is uncanny how the subconscious mind arranges "coincidences" and "opportunities" to steer you along your chosen path. Consider the story of the famous German rocket scientist Lothar von Blenk-Schmidt. During World War II, Blenk-Schmidt was sent as a prisoner of war to a Russian prison camp. He was ordered to mine 300 pounds of coal a day or see his meager ration cut, which would be certain death for him. His home and family wiped out, his associates killed or imprisoned, Blenk-Schmidt started thinking of escape and a brighter future in America. "I knew that my subconscious mind would somehow find a way... I said to my subconscious: 'I want to go to Los Angeles, and you will find the way.'" Recalling pictures he had seen, Blenk-Schmidt constantly visualized himself walking down LA's Wilshire Boulevard, visiting stores, riding buses and eating in restaurants. Soon, the warm mental pictures became as vividly real as the bleak scenery in the actual world around him. Then, one day, quite possibly through a synchronistic "coincidence," a chance came to escape. Because of a guard's counting error, Blenk-Schmidt was able to walk undetected out of the camp and get a lengthy head start on his captors. He hunted wildlife for food, stowed away on westward-moving nighttime coal trains, and eventually made it, with the help of friends, to neutral Switzerland. There, he met an American who invited him to visit his home in Santa Monica, Calif. "I found that (the American's chauffeur) drove me along Wilshire Boulevard and many other boulevards which I had imagined so vividly in the long months in the Russian coal mines. I recognized the buildings which I had seen in my mind so often. It actually seemed as if I had been in Los Angeles before." Joseph Murphy, who recounted the story in his book *The Power of Your Subconscious Mind*, quotes Blenk-Schmidt as concluding: "Truly it (the subconscious mind) has ways we know not of."

Another thing is certain about our individual subconscious blueprints, our "destinies." Those of us who have discovered our destinies, like Blenk-Schmidt, frequently show amazing faith and determination in achieving those futures, no matter the obstacles. In the late 1700s, a gypsy on the Caribbean island of Martinique prophesied to a girl named Josephine that she would one day become empress of France. So utterly convinced was Josephine of the prophecy that later, when she was jailed and threatened by the guillotine during the French Revolution, she defiantly told shouting prisoners that she would cheat the executioner and someday be queen of France.

## The Subconscious Creates Your Future

How did Josephine, starting on a Caribbean island, overcome all sorts of impediments and twists of fate to realize her future as Napoleon's consort? How did Blenk-Schmidt survive grueling work that killed so many and then penetrate hundreds of miles of hostile, unknown territory to realize his future? The answer, commentator after commentator agrees, lies with the creative power of the subconscious mind to "supernaturally" attract the conditions a person desires. Moreover, the subconscious mind prods you forward with helpful hunches and unexpected ideas.

For centuries, mystics have described the subconscious mind as an all-powerful creator of a person's reality. The subconscious shapes and molds an individual's reality until it perfectly mirrors his thinking about himself and his world. Unfortunately, the conscious mind, although the commander of the subconscious in this respect, is often weak, negative and vacillating in its thinking. So, the subconscious is like an all-powerful, wise genie taking orders from a far-from-perfect Aladdin (the conscious mind). This can wreak havoc, because the subconscious is constantly at work taking the bulk of a person's thoughts and translating that thinking into external physical conditions and circumstances.

"Hateful and condemnatory thoughts crystallize into habits of accusation and violence, which solidify into circumstances of injury and persecution," wrote Allen, giving one example of the process. "... loving and unselfish thoughts crystallize into habits of self-forgetfulness for others, which solidify into circumstances of sure and abiding prosperity and true riches." In the end, the subconscious mind will bring into your life the people and circumstances that exactly mirror your inner thinking, your inner spiritual condition. The subconscious will do this through logical cause-and-effect and through synchronistic "coincidences." This is, at the same time, an exhilarating and terrifying revelation.

"A man has but to right himself to find that the universe is right and during the process of putting himself right, he will find that as he alters his thoughts toward things and other people, things and other people will alter toward him," said Allen in his inspiring classic, *As A Man Thinketh*. The title comes from a Biblical proverb attributed to King Solomon: "As a man thinketh in his heart, so is he."

The mystics and their modern interpreters note that the subconscious mind is impersonal in what it creates. It always blindly and slavishly creates, in an all-powerful and never-failing way, according to the noble or base thoughts fed to it by the conscious mind. Where does the creative power of the subconscious come from? From the fact, many assert, that the subconscious is the supernatural bridge between an individual mind and the Cosmic Mind, the universal intelligence that created the universe and keeps it running.

## Poltergeists: The Creative Subconscious

Preposterous as the idea sounds that the subconscious could physically mold reality, this is exactly what many parapsychologists believe is happening in poltergeist cases. Most parapsychologists do not think that the poltergeist is actually a cantankerous spirit smashing dishes and overturning chairs. Rather, the majority of investigators thinks the phenomenon is caused by a living person unwittingly (subconsciously) using "psychokinesis," or mind over matter, to influence his physical environment. Very often, poltergeist activity breaks out in a house where a young adolescent harbors repressed anger, pushed out of the conscious mind to the subconscious. Fittingly, the poltergeist in the house smashes things, steals things and, in short, does the very things an enraged child would like to do but dares not do.

Poltergeist cases are well documented, although naturally controversial. For example, in November 1974, apparent poltergeist activity wrecked Gerald Goodin's residence in Bridgeport, Conn., author Scott Rogo noted in his 1978 book *Minds and Motion*, reporting on a *Los Angeles Times* article. The police brass labeled as a hoax the accounts of household articles moving by themselves. Over 40 persons went to the house, ranging from skeptics to dozens of witnesses, including officers, who said they watched as objects fell by themselves or flew through the air. These witnesses also included a priest who kept a vigil at the residence.

And mind-over-matter is apparently not even just a subconscious power. In the laboratory, the scientist Helmut Schmidt, mentioned earlier in this book, has appeared to demonstrate that persons can even **consciously** use psychokinesis (PK) to consistently skew what should be a random pattern of flashing lights in a computerized machine. Schmidt's findings are significant since his rigidly controlled experiments have won the grudging respect of hard-core skeptics.

## Artificial Poltergeist Created

Incidentally, in some cases, the poltergeist, drawing its psychokinetic power from a living subconscious mind, may even take on an intelligence and personality of its own. A bizarre and startling case of this was reported in the 1976 book *Conjuring Up Philip* by Iris Owen and Margaret Sparrow. Essentially, nine members of the Toronto Society for Psychical Research, including the wife of a poltergeist investigator, banded together to see if they could pool their subconscious minds to create an artificial ghost or poltergeist, "Philip." They invented a purely fictional personality and a biography for him and even took care to make some of the details of his life contrary to history. Among many other biographical details, they decided that the Philip they would create would be an English nobleman of the 1600s cheating on a frigid and negative wife, Dorothea, by consorting with a gypsy girl, Margo. Dorothea found out about the affair and had Margo wrongly burned at the stake as a witch. Philip was overcome with guilt for not having intervened to save Margo and committed suicide.

For months, the nine-member group met, meditating collectively on the idea of Philip. Some members started reporting feeling an invisible "presence" or catching purely mental glimpses of Philip. Eventually, seance-like table raps began. The sitters worked out a yes-no code of raps for Philip to use in communicating, and conversations began between an entity claiming to be Philip and the sitters. In his rap-mediated remarks, Philip stuck to the basic script for his life. But he emitted an unpleasant sawing noise, rather than any raps, if he was asked a biographical question which the group's script had not resolved for him. Philip displayed quite a personality. He made scratching noises when discussing his disagreeable wife Dorothea. He showed himself to be friendly, but moody and impatient. A joke-lover, he rattled the table when his fancy was tickled. But he was extremely sensitive to threats. Once, when one sitter warned a then-uncooperative Philip that the group could send him away if they wanted to, Philip got angry and "vanished" (fell silent). It took several hours of coaxing to get him to return.

Author Michael Talbot, who discussed the Philip case in his compelling 1988 book *Beyond the Quantum*, remarked that Philip's childishness and mischievousness bore an intriguing similarity to that of a poltergeist he himself had experienced as a youth. Indeed, investigators say one common feature of the poltergeist is its immature behavior.

Not content to merely rap, Philip also flickered the lights and moved the table, sometimes poising it up on one leg. Philip eventually got into the media eye, putting on live performances for Canadian TV studio audiences. During one live performance, Philip was apparently put off that he and his table had not been placed on a platform with other guests of the show. Amid general hilarity, Philip laboriously maneuvered his table up steps to the platform, while cameras filmed it all. The moderator then doubtfully placed his hand on the table, saying: "Hello, Philip." The studio was surprised by the immediate and loud answering rap, coming from right under the moderator's hand.

Philip, however, depended on the collective minds of his sitters. His ability to answer questions depended on who was present, and his preferences changed slightly if the make-up of the group changed. Talbot suggests that the individual consciousnesses of the sitters merged to form Philip's consciousness. Rogo observed: "The Philip work certainly proves that a group of people, none of whom are psychic, can develop startling PK abilities among themselves."

In summary, can the subconscious mind really use PK to literally shape reality and your future? The evidence from a variety of fronts suggests that this may well be so:

\*        The electronic PK experiments of Helmut Schmidt.

\*      The mind-over-matter phenomenon of the polter-geist. (In fact, Iris Owen called the Philip project "PK by committee." Some theorists believe that the seance atmosphere enabled the Canadian group to magnify their individually weak PK abilities.)

\*      The odd synchronistic "coincidences" that steer our lives.

\*      The centuries-old claims of mystics.

\*      The weird behavior of protons, electrons and other particles in the subatomic world, as described in the following section:

## The Mind and Subatomic Reality

In the 20th Century, physicists have joined mystics in asserting that the mind has a role in creating reality. Modern physicists have discovered that reality as we know it breaks down in the tiny world of protons, electrons and other subatomic particles. "Down there," everything has an unreal, ghostlike fuzziness. "Down there," you cannot say that a thing happened (such as that a particular uranium atom suddenly decayed into lead). You can only say that there is a probability that a thing would happen. (There is a certain probability that the uranium atom decayed into lead at a given moment and a certain probability that it didn't.) In fact, nothing about this little world, neither speed nor position nor other properties, is ever definite (i.e. real **unless and until** a thing is **observed** by a **knowing mind**. Until then, a thing half-exists in all of its possible states **simultaneously**, like a series of phantoms. (The uranium atom simultaneously remains uranium and decays into lead.) The simple act of observation, of looking with knowing eyes, causes the uranium atom, suddenly, to be either still uranium or decayed into lead. It is no longer "both and neither." The observed atom must suddenly "decide" which it is. One fuzzy possibility focuses into reality; the other is now excluded. In other words, our kind of "hard" reality is suddenly created out of the fuzziness of probabilities. The staggering implication of all this is that physics is saying, clearly and without hesitation, that reality "down there" depends on observing minds for its existence. In the words of Neils Bohr, a towering intellect of 20th

Century physics: "Anyone who is not shocked by quantum theory (what we've just discussed) has not understood it." As one writer cleverly noticed, our minds seem to be, in a sense, umpires of reality for the subatomic world: "Some is balls and some is strikes, but until I calls 'em, they ain't nothing," a major league umpire is supposed to have said.

If the mind is intimately involved in molding reality in the subatomic world, is the same thing happening in our larger world, many have justifiably asked in recent decades. After all, as one science writer noted: "Although quantum mechanics is accepted by the scientific world, this theory appears to hold that the universe around us has no form in itself until it is observed by beings with minds." In view of this, it is not so unreasonable to assert that your subconscious mind may be helping shape your future or that a Universal Mind may be carrying out a Grand Blueprint for our "coincidentally" hospitable cosmos. Is our incredibly fine-tuned universe, strangely perfect for human life, the result of mind-induced PK synchronicities, in the same way that the direction of a well-ordered individual life is steered by favorable synchronicities? (See *Destinies Larger Than Ours* later in this chapter).

## Is Time an Illusion?

Not just reality but even time itself may depend on the power of the mind. Mystics across cultures have contended for millennia that time's apparent flow from past through present into future is an illusion of our conscious minds, a tool used in our spiritual pilgrimages on earth. In fundamental reality, the past, present and future actually supposedly exist together in an all-encompassing "now." In the words of the Taoist sage Chuang Tzu, "Let us forget the lapse of time." Indeed, in recent years, persons brushing with death have reported experiencing a timelessness in the otherworldly realms they claimed to visit. And in other altered states of consciousness, such as dreams and hypnosis, the passage of time is known to become extremely relative. On another front, many physicists today are maintaining that in the miniscule fraction of a moment after the Big Bang, time and space did not yet even exist in the physical world, nor did cause-and-effect. Up until $10^{-43}$ second after the Big Bang, the newborn universe was "a non-place, in a non-time, 'where' there is never a reason for anything," wrote scientist John Gliedman, explaining the widely accepted scientific theory in his *Science Digest* article *Turning Einstein Upside Down*.

The scientist and precognitive dreamer, J. W. Dunne, theorized that the subconscious mind still sees reality in its true timelessness. To the subconscious mind, Dunne and others contend, the past, present and future are all displayed at once, like action frames of a movie film. It is only to the conscious mind that time seems to be a flowing river.

## Controlling the Subconscious

If the great mystics of history are right, if an all-powerful subconscious mind slavishly toils away creating a physical reality for us that mirrors our inner selves and inner thinking -- could we change our thinking and thus change our futures? If we discovered our blueprinted destinies through patient introspection, could we use the subconscious mind to bring our newfound destiny into existence?

The great inspirational author Napoleon Hill concluded, after decades of studying successful people, that the subconscious mind can be controlled and harnessed in fashioning a destiny. To harness the creative subconscious power, one changes deep-seated negative beliefs and attitudes about himself and his world into positive ones. As those beliefs and attitudes change, the subconscious changes one's reality to mirror the person's new favorable view of himself and the world around him. (The old, often negative beliefs had been haphazardly formed over a lifetime by careless self-suggestions and thoughtless opinions about the person and his world voiced by others and unfortunately accepted as true).

However, Hill said, the only known method for systematically changing deeply held beliefs is autosuggestion (self-suggestion). Typically, autosuggestion involves daily entering a relaxed but alert state, and vividly picturing in detail what you want already occurring in the present (in your imagination). You get the "strong feel" of what the realization of your goal is like. Meanwhile, you "see" its accomplishment vividly in your mind's eye. You imagine all this happening in the present. This visualization may be accompanied by a verbal, emotion-charged affirmation (self-suggestion), such as, "I radiate a loving, self-confidence that attracts others." The preceding self-suggestion might be repeated, perhaps, by a timid and lonely person. The person seeks to change a deep, negative self-image or belief. When the negative belief fades in favor of a positive one, his subconscious mind will alter both him and, thus, the world around him. Hill and a chorus of others note that the self-suggestion and visualization should be highly charged with faith, since emotions are the "fuel" for affecting the subconscious. The very relaxed and highly alert state, incidentally, helps you bypass your often negative conscious mind and its self-limiting beliefs, to reach the impressionable subconscious. Once your inner emotions and beliefs have switched from negative to positive, the subconscious mind can become an awesome ally of yours, supplying you with endless ideas for action to achieve your goals, bolstering you emotionally, even arranging helpful "coincidences." In a larger vein, the subconscious will be busy improving your outer world to mirror your improved inner world of thought and emotion.

"You are a gardener, and you are planting seeds (thoughts) in your subconscious mind all day long, based on your habitual thinking. As you sow in your subconscious mind, so shall you reap in your body and environment..." observed Murphy. Hill and other commentators suggest a systematic plan (visualization and emotionalized self-instructions) to sow the right thought-seeds in the subconscious and root out the "weeds" (harmful, limiting beliefs).

Or, in Allen's words, a person "can only rise, conquer and achieve by lifting up his thoughts. He can only remain weak and abject and miserable by refusing to lift up his thoughts." People "do not attract that which they **want** but that which they **are**." (i.e, in their attitudes, thinking and beliefs)."

In recent years, techniques for affecting the creative subconscious have gained widespread acceptance in the business community, simply because they appear to work. Moreover, these ideas conform to age-old religious traditions from around the world:

\*       "You will decree a thing, and it will be established for you."
        (The Old Testament *Book of Job*)

151

* "When you pray and ask for something, believe that you have received it, and you will be given whatever you ask for." (Jesus of Nazareth)
* "When the mind rests steady and pure, then whatever you desire, those desires are fulfilled. (The Hindu *Upanishads*)
* "Can you walk on water? You have done no better than a straw. Can you fly in the air? You have done no better than a bluebottle fly. Conquer your heart (mind); then you may become somebody." (Ansari of Herat)

## Destinies Larger Than Ours

If individuals have subconscious blueprints for their lives, do entire nations have blueprinted destinies, the whole human race, even the universe itself? One top scientist has suggested that a hierarchy of minds could exist, reaching down from the Universal Mind through intermediate but awesomely powerful minds indistinguishable from nature, to us. Is each level of mind working out its own destiny? In recent years, scientists have been turning up more and more startling data to indicate that this universe of ours, and this planet of ours, may be far from accidental. Increasingly, both of them appear to be the products of design, perhaps by "universal" and planet-wide "minds."

As for the universe, scientists have discovered a multitude of freaky coincidences in nature which have worked together to bring about a universe suitable for intelligent human life. The strength of gravity is just right, the strength of the force holding atomic nucleuses together is just right, the force of the explosive Big Bang was just right, the universe's age is just right, and on and on and on. And very often, had one or another of these things varied by the minutest of degrees either way, a chain-reaction of ominous consequences would have been set off. These consequences would have made our universe incapable of allowing intelligent human life to arise, scientists now know with their computer calculations. To take just one of many examples, had the Big Bang's explosiveness deviated by an infinitesimal 1 part in $10^{60}$ (1 followed by 60 zeros), a universe supportive of intelligent human life would not have developed, according to scientist Paul Davies. In his 1983 book *God*

152

*and the New Physics*, Davies said that, with this kind of precision, a sharpshooter could successfully hit a one-inch target 20 billion light years away -- at the opposite end of the observable universe. Davies comments: "It is hard to resist the impression that the present structure of the universe, apparently so sensitive to minor alterations in the numbers, has been rather carefully thought out..." Davies adds that "the seeming miraculous concurrence of numerical values that nature has assigned to her fundamental constants must remain the most compelling evidence for an element of cosmic design." As another commentator put it, to say that an incredibly fine-tuned universe like ours arose without a blueprint, by accident, would be like saying that an explosion at a print shop accidentally produced a mistake-proof Encyclopedia Britainnica. But as the TV character Archie Bunker once pointed out, "God don't make no mistakes. That's how he got to be God."

Similarly, numerous coincidences have also been noticed in the history of earth's evolution. These many coincidences have made it possible for, first, life and then intelligent life to arise here. With growing evidence to back him, the maverick scientist James E. Lovelock has theorized that all living things on earth, from humans to amoebas, act together like an intelligent superorganism, a huge living creature. This seeming planetary intelligence has kept all living things exquisitely cooperating to deliberately produce a planet optimal for our kind of life and to keep it that way, despite all kinds of outside forces. For example, over four billion years, the sun has grown much hotter, yet surface temperatures on earth have not correspondingly increased, thanks to the activity of the earth's ecosystems. Another of many examples: For billions of years, the oceans' salt content has stayed roughly around 3.4 percent, despite the constant flow of salt into oceans through rivers. If the saltiness had ever reached four percent, a very different evolution of life would have occurred. At just over six percent, all ocean life would be wiped out in minutes. Or take oxygen. If the atmosphere's content of oxygen were just a bit lower than the 21 percent it has been for hundreds of millions of years, larger animals would not have the energy to exist. If the oxygen content were just a little higher, vegetation would burn so easily that forest fires would rage out of control and soon, all the planet's vegetation would be burned up. In this so-called Gaia

Hypothesis (named for the ancient Greek goddess of the earth, Gaia), the planet is seen to resemble a self-organizing beehive, with the individual cooperating bees comparable to the cooperating life forms on earth. Yet, an overall intelligence of some sort directs the entire hive and all the bees so that they work together in startling precision.

## Free Will vs. Predestination

In all this may lie the answer to the age-old debate over whether human beings have the free will to chart their own futures or whether we are trapped into following, like robots, a preordained plan of events. The Anthropic Principle (the coincidences surrounding the universe) and the Gaia Hypothesis suggest that larger intelligences may be at work with their own grand plans and destinies, and our little lives must go with that flow. However, although we must conform to the Big Picture, we are allowed generous freedom in ordering the many details of our individual lives. In the same way, the disease-fighting white blood cell coursing through your veins has its own destiny but that destiny is caught up, naturally, with yours. The Victorian writer William Henley is apparently still basically right in saying: "I am the master of my fate. I am the captain of my soul."

## The Grand Blueprint and Us

Whatever our blueprinted destinies may be, as we discover and fulfill them, we may realize that they fit snugly into the Creator's larger picture, as visionaries have long claimed. Our fulfilled destinies just "happen" to benefit everyone and further the Grand Blueprint. The closer our destinies fit the Creator's will and plans, the greater our satisfaction and triumph in life, the thinking goes. Jesus of Nazareth may have been considering all this when he prayed in anguish, shortly before his arrest, in Jerusalem's Garden of Gethsemane. Jesus prayed that his soon-to-come "cup of suffering" be removed from his personal destiny. But in the end, he told the Supreme Creator he was willing to serve the larger picture, no matter the cost: "Not my will, but yours," he said. Or consider how the ancient Indian prince Gautama sacrificed to further the larger divine plan. His royal father had bequeathed to him a self-indulgent, luxurious lifestyle. According to tradition, in 533 B.C., the young prince came upon a sick man, an aged man, and a corpse. After seeing them, the pampered Gautama became deeply aware that suffering was the common condition of humanity. Yet Gautama also encountered a begging monk who despite his poverty had peace of mind and happiness. Gautama decided to sacrifice his wealth and opulent palace life. The idealistic prince dedicated his life to determining the cause of human suffering and how to cure it. His long quest for answers as a wandering holy man finally brought him superhuman enlightenment and the title "The Buddha" (The Enlightened One). The Buddha's sacrifice of a life of luxury, the beginning of his higher mission, is called the "Great Renunciation" and is considered a turning point in history by the world's hundreds of millions of Buddhists. Our blueprinted destinies may not be as drastic as the Christ's or the Buddha's, but sacrifice does stand between us and their realization -- as part of the larger plan, according to this way of thinking.

By contrast, if we neglect the whispered, intuitive call of our best destinies, whether humble or exalted, we can avoid the sacrifices. However, we end up sacrificing more in the frustration and unhappiness that come from missing our callings.

Sometimes, our perceived destiny looks hopelessly unattainable. Yet, we grossly underestimate our abilities. Hypnosis and emergencies which summon subconscious power prove that only the tiniest fraction of our potential is realized on an everyday basis. Persons in the deepest states of hypnosis -- where concentration is nearly absolute -- have demonstrated virtual total recall and otherwise displayed incredible physical and mental prowess. Dare to achieve your best destiny and watch your capabilities rise with your efforts and sacrifices. Smile at the "coincidences" that begin to aid you at every turn. As the great philosopher Emerson put it: "Do the deed, and you will have the power." Or in the words of Jesus of Nazareth: "Ask, and you will receive. Seek, and you will find. Knock, and the door will be opened for you."

We are not accustomed to thinking that the Supreme Creator needs our help in furthering his Master Plan, which has already brought the universe from protons to philosophers in 20 billion years. In fact, major religions agree that the Creator does need self-actualized individuals who have gone beyond mere coping and survival to thriving, so that they can begin helping others rise. The fulfillment of the world's destiny starts with the fulfilled destinies of individual persons: "Let there be peace on earth, and let it begin with me," goes the oft-sung hymn, giving one example of the process.

## Illusion of Separateness

Physicists say that at the universe's most basic level of reality, on the subatomic plane, nothing is truly separated from anything else. Everything is interconnected, interdependent, and united. Indeed, mystics have always said that the separateness of our world is an illusion of the senses. The universe, they say, is actually one united, living organism, its parts exquisitely coordinated so that each acts ultimately for the best future of all the parts.

According to this view, the many parts of the universe all work out their best destinies in a coordinated, teamwork precision. This is much like the one quadrillion cells of the human body harmonizing in their individual efforts to support a larger, living whole. Each cell is quite unaware of the Grand Blueprint: You and your larger destiny. If part of the body thrives or suffers, the rest of the body is affected. Yet, each cell is technically a separate living thing. As the famous English poet John Donne put it, "No man is an island... Any man's death diminishes me... and, therefore, never send to know for whom the (funeral) bell tolls; It tolls for thee."

Napoleon Hill once said he could imagine that the angels of heaven sing when a person finally finds himself. The discovery of your individual destiny can unleash tremendous untapped powers within you as you help yourself and your world rise. As Jesus told his disciples, men who had found their own earthly destinies, destinies which also dovetailed with the Cosmic Plan: "Greater things than I do will you do." In fact, the long steady march of progress by the universe indicates that our self-awakenings are just a matter of time. As Paul of Tarsus wrote 2,000 years ago: "He (the Creator) who has begun a good work in you will see it to completion."

# Bibliography

## Books

Allen, James. *As a Man Thinketh*. Grosset & Dunlap, N.Y. 1984. This warm and insightful book should be universally read. Allen has powerfully conveyed in a brief little book the awesome power of the mind and the beautiful laws of the universe. Intensely inspiring.

*Arthur C. Clarke's World of Strange Powers*. G. P. Putnam's Sons, N.Y. 1984. A general survey of the psychic field.

Bartlett, Laile. *Psi-Trek*. McGraw-Hill Book Co., N.Y. 1981. With a sociologist's perspective, Bartlett concisely summarizes the widely varying doings of the psychic world.

Bentov, Itzhak. *Stalking the Wild Pendulum*. E.P. Dutton, N.Y. 1977. Bentov presents a bizarre but plausible picture of what reality is like, beyond the illusory world of our senses.

Bucke, Richard. *Cosmic Consciousness*. Innes & Sons. 1901. The who, what, where, when and why of universal consciousness. Bucke has written a substantial book. He even supplies a list of historical figures who he suspects had cosmic consciousness.

Calkins, Carroll, project ed. *Reader's Digest Mysteries of the Unexplained*. Reader's Digest Association. 1982.

Capra, Fritjof. *The Tao of Physics*. Bantam Books, N.Y. 1977. Capra clearly examines the latest discoveries of physics and shows how they tend to confirm the ancient ideas of mystics about the nature of the world. An established favorite.

Cavendish, Richard, ed. *Man, Myth and Magic*. Marshall Cavendish Corp., N.Y. 1970.

Davies, Paul. *God and the New Physics*. Simon and Schuster, N.Y. 1983.

Ebon, Martin. *Prophecy in Our Time*. New American Library, N.Y. 1968. Ebon thoughtfully surveys precognition in a general way, adding a psychological viewpoint missing in some other works.

Edwards, Frank. *Strangest of All*. New American Library, N.Y. 1974.

Edwards, I.G. *Second Sight*. Thomas Nelson, Nashville, Tenn. 1977.

Eisenbud, Jule. *Paranormal Foreknowledge*. Human Sciences Press, N.Y. 1982.

Fisher, Joe, with Peter Commins. *Predictions*. Van Nostrand Reinhold Co., N.Y. 1980.

Fodor, Nandor. *The Encyclopedia of Psychic Science*. Citadel Press, Secaucus, N.J. An exhaustive treasury of facts by a tireless researcher.

Forman, Henry J. *The Story of Prophecy*. Farrar and Reinhart, N.Y. 1936.

Garrett, Eileen. *The Sense and Nonsense of Prophecy*. Berkeley Publishing Corp. 1968. Garrett recounts the fraudulent as well as the seemingly legitimate in the psychic world.

Garrison, Omar. *The Encyclopedia of Prophecy*. Citadel Press, Secaucus, N.J. 1978. A general work.

Glass, Justine. *They Foresaw the Future*. G. P. Putnam's Sons, N.Y. 1969.

Greenhouse, Herbert. *Premonitions: A Leap into the Future*. Warner Books, N.Y. 1973. A fact-filled, general look at precognition.

Hall, Angus and King, Francis. *Mysteries of Prediction*. Aldus Books, London. 1975.

Harman, Willis. *Global Mind Change*. Knowledge Systems, Indianapolis, Ind. 1988. Harman comprehensively and lucidly argues that this generation is seeing a fundamental shift in the world view of Western culture. Namely, the decline of materialistic and mechanistic ideas about the universe.

Huxley, Aldous. Harper and Row, N.Y. 1944. *The Perennial Philosophy*. A classic work by the famous novelist (*Brave New World*) and critic. Huxley contends that all major religions are actually united in their intuitive, mystical teachings, although their official, rationalist dogmas may differ fantastically. Huxley calls this surprising, agreed-upon theology "the perennial philosophy."

James, William. *The Varieties of Religious Experience*. New American Library, N.Y. 1958. A classic by the turn-of-the-century philosopher on the many different ways of spiritual seeking.

Koestler, Arthur. *The Roots of Coincidence*. Random House, N.Y. A look at coincidence and synchronicity.

Leoni, Edgar. *Nostradamus and his Prophecies*. Bell Publishing Co., N.Y. 1982. Leoni's scholarly yet interestingly written approach to this endlessly fascinating seer is like a breath of fresh air. His conservative, no-nonsense scrutiny casts serious doubts on some of the more extravagant claims made by popular writers about Nostradamus. Yet Leoni also finds much in Nostradamus' enigmatic *Centuries* to be impressed about. Nostradamus buffs should enjoy this book.

Lewinsohn, Richard. *Science, Prophecy and Prediction*. Harper and Brothers, N.Y. 1961.

Lovelock, J.E. *Gaia: A New Look at Life on Earth*. Oxford University Press, Oxford. 1979. A discussion by Lovelock of his landmark theory that a kind of planetary intelligence regulates the ecosystems of earth.

MacKenzie, Andrew. *Riddle of the Future*. Taplinger Publishing Co., N.Y. 1974.

Mishlove, Jeffrey. *The Roots of Consciousness*. Random House, N.Y. 1975. An encyclopedic treatment of numerous topics relating to metaphysics and consciousness.

Murphy, Joseph. *The Power of Your Subconscious Mind*. Bantam Books, N.Y. 1982. An outstanding and absorbing examination of how the subconscious controls your individual reality and how it may be influenced to improve your reality. A continual backlist favorite.

*Mysteries of the Unknown: Visions and Prophecies*. Time-Life Books, Alexandria, Va. A thorough overview. Strengths of the book include its balanced approach to controversial themes and its clearing up of some longheld inaccuracies in the field. Lavish illustrations give a new dimension to the prose. Recommended.

*Mysteries of the Unknown: Cosmic Connections*. Time-Life Books. Alexandria, Va. Similar in journalistic quality to its companion volume above but dealing with the subject of astrology.

Peat, F. David. *Synchronicity: The Bridge Between Matter and Mind*. Bantam Books, N.Y. 1987. Peat discusses the connection between quantum physics and synchronicity. He combines anecdotes, scientific analysis, observations of the natural world, and the thought of leading scientists and philosophers. Recommended for serious students of meaningful coincidence.

Petrie, Sidney. *What Modern Hypnotism Can Do for You*. Fawcett Crest, Greenwich, Conn. 1972. A detailed and interesting survey of the subject from many different angles.

Rogo, D. Scott. *Minds and Motion*. Taplinger Publishing Co., N.Y. 1978. A journalist surveys the subject of psychokinesis (mind-over-matter), including PK's suspected role in poltergeist phenomena. As usual, Rogo is thorough, clear and interesting.

Russell, Peter. *The Global Brain*. J.P. Tarcher, Los Angeles. 1983. Russell obviously put a lot of effort into this book. He discusses the idea that living things on earth may all be part of a superorganism regulating the planet. And he broaches the intriguing idea that humanity may act as this organism's brain.

Schultz, Ted, ed. *The Fringes of Reason*. Harmony Books, N.Y. 1989.

Shephard, Leslie, ed. *Encyclopedia of Occultism and Parapsychology*. Gale Research Co., Detroit. 1985.

Sherman, Harold. *How to Make ESP Work for You*.

Stearn, Jess. *Edgar Cayce: The Sleeping Prophet*. Bantam Books, N.Y. 1968.

Talbot, Michael. *Beyond the Quantum: How the Secrets of the New Physics are Bridging the Chasm Between Science and Faith*. Bantam Books, N.Y. 1988. A delightful and mind-expanding book with a self-explanatory title. Don't miss this one.

Vaughan, Alan. *Patterns of Prophecy*. Hawthorn Books, N.Y. 1973. Vaughan develops here the idea of synchronicity in prophecy, among other novel approaches. All of Vaughan's books on precognition are marked by good content, readability and sensitivity. Many of his books' original insights stem from the simple fact that he is a practicing prophet himself.

-------. *The Edge of Tomorrow*. Coward, McCann & Geoghegan, N.Y. 1982.

-------*Incredible Coincidence: The Baffling World of Synchronicity*. J. B. Lippincott Co., N.Y. 1979. Vaughan collects various anecdotes about synchronistic happenings.

Wallace, Amy and Wallechinsky, David. *The Book of Predictions*. William Morrow & Co., N.Y. 1980. An avalanche of information about prophecy and precognition crammed into one volume.

Wallace, Irving and Wallechinsky, David. *The People's Almanac 2*. Bantam Books, New York. 1978. A 1,422-page smorgasbord of colorful information for the reader.

Watson, Lyall. *Supernature*. Anchor Press/Doubleday, Garden City, N.Y. 1973.

Wilson, Colin. *The Occult: A History*. Random House, N.Y. 1971.

*World Almanac Book of the Strange 1*. New American Library, N.Y. 1977.

*World Almanac Book of the Strange 2*. New American Library, N.Y. 1982.

# Articles

Earley, George. *The Stamp That Foretold the Future*. Fate. August 1988.

Gardner, Martin. *Quantum Weirdness*. Discover. October 1982.

Melton, J. Gordon. *Living in the New Age*. Fate. August and September 1987.

Rothman, Tony. *A What You See is What You Beget Theory*. Discover. May 1987. A fine discussion of the cosmic *anthropic* coincidences that have made some scientists wonder if we live in a "designer universe."

Wilson, Robert A. *Mere Coincidence*. Science Digest. January 1982. A absorbing capsule look at the phenomena of synchronicity.

*World Healing Day*. Science of Mind. December 1988.

# Appendix

## Organizations of Interest

**American Society for Psychical Research.** 5 W. 73rd St., New York, N.Y. 10023. Organized in 1885, this 2,000-member organization investigates the whole field of the paranormal, including precognition. ASPR also maintains a 9,000-volume library on psychical research and publishes a quarterly newsletter and a research journal.

**Millennium Society.** 6000 Ranleigh Manor, McLean, Va. 22101. This 1,100-member international group was founded in 1969 and is devoted to promoting peace and to specially celebrating the coming of the new millennium in the year 2,000. The society publishes the quarterly *Millennium* magazine as well as a quarterly newsletter.

**Titanic Historical Society.** P.O. Box 51053, Indian Orchard, Mass. 01151. This group concerns itself with the history of the Titanic and lore surrounding the ship and the 1912 tragedy, including survivor stories. The organization publishes *The Titanic Communicator*, a quarterly journal carrying book reviews, among other things.

**World Future Society.** 4916 St. Elmo Ave., Bethesda, Md. 20814. Active since the mid-1960s, the futurist WFS boasts 30,000 members interested in a logical and rationalist study of the future. It sponsors a book service, maintains a library and offers a specialized education program.

# Index

167

# Acknowledgments

I would like to thank the staff of the Jacksonville State University library in Jacksonville, Ala., particularly Deborah Thompson; the staffs of the Anniston, Ala. and Oxford, Ala. public libraries; and Jeanne Hoechst-Ronner for their unstinting and cheerful readiness to help with this demanding project.

# Production Notes

*Seeing Your Future* was written on a Hyundai Super 286C AT-compatible computer using Word Star 2000 Plus Version 3 word processing software. Typesetting was done with an Epson EPL-6000 laser printer. Screening and sizing of prints and photographs was provided by Moore Printing and Higginbotham Printers of Anniston, Ala. Offset printing and perfect binding was by McNaughton & Gunn of Ann Arbor, Mich. The cover was designed by Tim Hartsfield.

# Picture Credits

Pages 22 and 24: Library of Congress
Page 116, upper left: Culver Pictures

# Do You Have A Guardian Angel?

John Ronner's first book, *Do You Have A Guardian Angel?*, received national attention, including favorable reviews in *Library Journal* and *The Washington Times*. The book, now in a third printing, contains hundreds of facts, stories, quotes and figures about angels: ghostly armies, deathbed visions, famous witnesses, supernatural rescues and more! Here's just a sampling of the questions you'll find discussed in the book: * Who's who in heaven and hell? * Do angels escort the newly dead to the Beyond? * How many angels can dance on the point of a pin? * What are fallen angels? * What are some spectacular cases of angel rescues? * Do angels secretly run the machinery of the universe? * Do angels keep a record of every good and bad deed we commit?

**What Others Are Saying:**

"Ronner's 'Guardian Angels' is hard to put down" -- **Florida Today**

"Fascinating" -- **Syndicated columnist Alan Caruba**

"Highly recommending John Ronner's book" -- **Spiritual Frontiers Fellowship Newsletter**

"Myriad visionaries have written (the author) of their experiences" -- **Birmingham News**

*Guardian Angel* tackles the basic questions: **Do powerful guardian spirits protect and guide you in your struggles? When you die, will an angel be there to lead you? Are higher powers gradually guiding our world to greater heights?**

* 5 1/2 X 8 1/2 Softcover * ISBN 0-932945-37-6 * 31 full-page illustrations * 194 pages * Bibliography * Index * $10.95

      **Guarantee:** You must be satisfied or your money back.

*************************************************************

Yes, please send me _____ copies of *Guardian Angel* at $10.95 each. I'm enclosing a check or money order. If I am not delighted with the book, I may return it within 30 days for a full, quick refund.

**Mail to: Mamre Press, 1301 Sherwood, Oxford AL 36203**

Name_____

Address_____

City _____ State _____ Zip _____

# See Your Future;

# Find and Fulfill Your Destiny

Is it *really* possible to foresee your future? Does <u>everyone</u> have at least latent prophetic powers? Do you have a sub-conscious plan for your life? And is there a cosmic plan into which our destinies all fit? Journalist John Ronner, (author of the nationally reviewed 1985 book **Do You Have a Guardian Angel?**) spent two years researching these questions and others. The result is a popularly written, heavily il-lustrated 185-page book: *Seeing Your Future*. This fascinat-ing new book delves into the subject of prophecy and foreseeing the future from **nearly every conceivable angle**. *Seeing Your Future* looks at the great seer Nostradamus, astrology, divination, trend-projecting futurists and what they see ahead for us, famous soothsayers of history, prophetic dreams, the millennialist doomsday debate (do we face a nuclear Armageddon or a peaceful Age of Aquarius or neither?), and much more. The book also discusses:

\* Evidence that *everyone* has prophetic powers and uses them, although the use is unconscious with most of us.

\* Evidence that **each of us has a subconscious plan for our lives, known to our inner selves, to be gradually discovered and fulfilled.**

\* Recent scientific discoveries which suggest that our planet and our universe may be the products of a <u>grand design</u>, rather than chaotic chance.

\*\*\*\*\*\*\*\*\*\*\*\*\*\*\*\*\*\*\*\*\*\*\*\*\*\*\*\*\*\*\*\*\*\*\*\*\*\*\*\*\*\*\*\*\*\*\*\*\*\*\*\*\*\*\*\*\*\*\*\*

Yes, please send me _____ copies of *Seeing Your Future* at $10.95 each. I enclose a check or money order. If I am not delighted with the book, I may return it within 30 days for a full, quick refund.

**Mail to: Mamre Press, 1301 Sherwood, Oxford AL 36203**

Name _____

Address _____

City _____ State ____ Zip _____

# Free Information About Books
# From Mamre Press

For FREE information about *all* books available from Mamre Press, just fill out and mail the coupon below. The information will be mailed to you promptly.

\*\*\*\*\*\*\*\*\*\*\*\*\*\*\*\*\*\*\*\*\*\*\*\*\*\*\*\*\*\*\*\*\*\*\*\*\*\*\*\*\*\*\*\*\*\*\*\*\*\*\*\*\*\*\*\*\*\*\*\*\*\*\*\*

Yes, please send me FREE information about all books available from Mamre Press. I obtained a copy of *Seeing Your Future* at:

_____

**Mail to: Mamre Press, 1301 Sherwood, Oxford AL 36203**

Name_____

Address_____

City _____ State _____ Zip _____